Catching Tigers in Red Weather

Catching Tigers in Red Weather

Imaginative Writing and Student

Choice in High School

Judith Rowe Michaels

Princeton Day School

Foreword by
Tom Romano

National Council of Teachers of English
1111 W. Kenyon Road, Urbana, Illinois 61801-1096

Staff Editor: Bonny Graham
Interior Design: Barbara Yale-Read
Cover Design: Barbara Yale-Read

NCTE Stock Number: 04651

It is the policy of NCTE in its journals and other publications to provide a forum for the open discussion of ideas concerning the content and the teaching of English and the language arts. Publicity accorded to any particular point of view does not imply endorsement by the Executive Committee, the Board of Directors, or the membership at large, except in announcements of policy, where such endorsement is clearly specified.

Every effort has been made to provide current URLs and email addresses, but because of the rapidly changing nature of the Web, some sites and addresses may no longer be accessible.

Library of Congress Cataloging-in-Publication Data
Michaels, Judy Rowe, 1944–
   Catching tigers in red weather : imaginative writing and student choice in high school/ Judith Rowe Michaels.
       p.   cm.
   Includes bibliographical references.
   ISBN 978-0-8141-0465-1 (pbk.)
 1. Creative writing (Secondary education) I. Title.
   LB1631.M445 2011
   808'.0420712—dc23

                                                         2011033109

*For Kate, long-time friend and colleague
who knows the joys and perils of catching tigers
in red weather*

Disillusionment of Ten o'Clock

The houses are haunted
By white night-gowns.
None are green,
Or purple with green rings,
Or green with yellow rings,
Or yellow with blue rings,
None of them are strange,
With socks of lace
And beaded ceintures.
People are not going
To dream of baboons and periwinkles.
Only, here and there, an old sailor,
Drunk and asleep in his boots,
Catches tigers
In red weather.

Wallace Stevens

Contents

Foreword

*I*f you're holding this book, you're likely a hungry English teacher. Consider what you're reading now the appetizer for the feast ahead. Halfway through reading *Catching Tigers in Red Weather*, I jotted this:

> I want legislators to read this book. Judy Michaels shows them a master English teacher at work, one with wisdom about teenagers and how they learn, a deep understanding of reading and writing, a nimble mind, a clear eye, and sense of humor.

Little likelihood of catching those readers, and I'm probably pipe-dreaming about the effect it would have on them. The ones who will relish the craft and moxie of this book are those who became hooked on language and literature and have dedicated their lives to teaching others to read and write. They are, I know, ravenous. For them, *Catching Tigers* holds ideas that are philosophical, political, and practical.

Judy's words were excellent repast for me—this former high school teacher and current English education professor. I am eager to share *Catching Tigers* with my undergraduates. The author demonstrates how she gives

> . . . *all* students experience in creative writing within the context of a standard literature curriculum . . . and how those genres that they study

as texts but are rarely taught to write . . . give them access to strategies
that can enliven all their writing, including the analytical essay, with its
emphasis on argument and persuasion.

My college students will quicken to that quote. Many of them have been
invigorated by writing narrative and poetry but numbed by producing
countless academic essays about literature—always, it seems, thesis-driven
and formulaic (i.e., the five paragraph you-know-what), not at all what
Montaigne had in mind when he fathered the essay more than 400 years
ago.

One sheer pleasure of this book is the quality of the language in it—the
language of the literature students read, the language of these developing
high school writers and readers, and the language of the author, a word
woman par excellence. Good writers, Judy Michaels knows, are honest
and know about living, leaping words. "I hasten to assure [students]," she
writes, "that there is no single 'right' way for a poem to take shape, any
more than an essay or story has to start from an outline bristling with
Roman numerals." With one well-chosen word, Judy evokes the fierceness
that academic essays hold for many people. On page after page of *Catching
Tigers,* you'll encounter surprises of language and thinking that stir your
pedagogical spirit.

Judy acknowledges that her students will someday encounter timed
essay tests and expectations of proficient writing "for an audience of speed-
reading adults counting up pieces of 'supporting evidence . . . .'" We can
debate whether such a genre really demonstrates writing proficiency, but
there the hurdle stands, nevertheless. How, Judy asks, "should we, the
writing teachers, motivate our students to learn the skills for this peculiar
task?"

The answer she has come to after years of teaching is to "help kids learn
to enjoy writing for itself, to approach it as an art like music or Web design
or moviemaking that engages their individual imaginations and lets them
say something that matters to them."

In writing assignments bound to the novel, essays, poems, and play
they are reading, students write profiles of each other, for which they learn
interviewing techniques and how to choose revealing quotations. They
render a time when they were "in the zone," so psychologically engaged in
some activity that they were unaware of the passage of time, the challenge

here to describe a mental and emotional state with evocative detail. They write a piece in the voice and style of a novel they've read and reread. They write analysis and argument that grow out of a troubling experience—an occasion when they fell short in some way. They write poetry. And as the semester finale, they write in a genre of their own choosing.

When completing recommendations, I often encounter this yes or no question: "Would you want this applicant to teach your child?" Teach my child? I wish Judy Michaels had taught me! She teaches adolescents to dig deep with language and discover what they think, to read with alertness and sensitivity—routine habits of mind for those who write. This drive she has to teach students sophisticated literacy skills is folded within a philosophy that urges adolescents to live this sweet life well. Of the "in the zone" assignment, she writes

> I want [students] to recognize and value the joy of "losing" themselves in something, of living in the moment. I don't want their education to be focused on the next term grade, standardized test, college transcript, career. They'll meet these future events naturally and as successfully as their trained abilities allow. . . . I'm with John Dewey: education should be a continuous process of growth, not simply preparation.

You'll lose yourself, blissfully, in *Catching Tigers*. Teaching is an optimal psychological experience for Judy. She describes, she explains, she reasons, she imagines. The students work; she works—works smart—but works hard. This book is not about how to handle the paper load or proficiency test prep. It is about teaching adolescents to write with control *and* abandon, to deepen their understanding of how language and genre work, to write with the eye of a reporter and the heart of a novelist.

Catching Tigers reminds us that we are humanities teachers. We believe in the art of language, in the rigor required to learn to use it well. We believe in the whole student. We believe that learning to be literate is a long process that involves much more than bristling core standards:

> [A]s a teacher of the art and craft of writing, I'd like to help produce not only future employees in the global economy but also imaginative friends, siblings, lovers, neighbors, grown sons and daughters, and parents of imaginative teenagers.

Judy Michaels has set a sumptuous table for you. Sit, please. Break this bread of excellent literacy teaching. There is sustenance here and complex flavors you'll savor. You'll learn. You'll reflect. Your hunger to teach will grow.

Tom Romano
Miami University
Oxford, Ohio

Permission Acknowledgments

WE GRATEFULLY ACKNOWLEDGE THE PUBLISHERS WHO GENEROUSLY GAVE US PERMISSION TO REPRODUCE THE FOLLOWING MATERIALS:

"Disillusionment of Ten O'Clock" from THE COLLECTED POEMS OF WALLACE STEVENS by Wallace Stevens, copyright 1954 by Wallace Stevens and renewed 1982 by Holly Stevens. Used by permission of Alfred A. Knopf, a division of Random House, Inc.

"Eye-to-Eye" from *Words under the Words: Selected Poems* by Naomi Shihab Nye, copyright © 1995. Reprinted with the permission of Far Corner Books, Portland, Oregon.

Lines from "Charlie Howard's Descent" from *Turtle Swan* by Mark Doty. Reprinted by permission of David R. Godine, Publisher, Inc. Copyright © 1987 by Mark Doty.

The lines from "anyone lived in a pretty how town" . Copyright 1940, © 1968, 1991 by the Trustees for the E. E. Cummings Trust, from COMPLETE POEMS: 1904–1962 by E. E. Cummings, edited by George J. Firmage. Used by permission of Liveright Publishing Corporation.

Selections from "Blood" from *Words under the Words: Selected Poems* by Naomi Shihab Nye, copyright © 1995. Reprinted with the permission of Far Corner Books, Portland, Oregon.

Acknowledgments

My thanks to Princeton Day School for granting me a sabbatical in 2009–10 to draft this book; to Lois Harrod, teacher, poet, and friend, for formatting the manuscript; to the PDS English department, an inspiring group of teachers and writers with whom it's a joy to share and fine-tune ideas about how to teach writing, and particularly to my longtime collaborator in shaping a grade 9 writing curriculum, Kate Winton, to whom this book is dedicated. I owe a great deal to the ninth graders whose writing and speaking voices helped bring this book to life and from whom I learned so much, particularly about the value of the three-week free-choice writing project and the virtues of entrusting students with the responsibility for helping to create criteria for assessing, revising, and grading the writing they produce. And last, deep gratitude to my late husband, Bill, always my first reader and often my most discriminating critic.

Chapter 1

Feeding the Imagination

Introduction, Draft A

As teachers of English or language arts, we know what we mean when we say "creative writing"—fiction, poetry, drama, maybe creative nonfiction or personal narrative, too—the literary genres, or as some people say, "frills." I heard that last word a lot growing up, when during dinner my father, the school music teacher, would fulminate over editorials in our small-town newspaper that attacked the school budget for wasting money on "frills" like music and art. "A new piano for the auditorium? A second music teacher? What do they think this is, a music school?"

That was the 1950s. Today, with the addition of state tests to the SAT, ACT, and AP exams, and the prevalence of scripted lesson plans, there is even less patience with "frills." Like the other arts, creative writing is increasingly cut from high school programs or, at best, relegated to a minor that meets just a couple of times a week and is designed either for the specially gifted or the non-college-prep students. We're told it doesn't look impressive on transcripts and is viewed as an easy pass. When I began this book, in 2008, the Language Arts Literacy Standards in my home state of New Jersey expected graduating seniors to be able to write "a range of essays and expository pieces" and "a literary research paper" but made no mention of poetry, fiction, drama—or, for that matter, imagination. (While thoughtful distinctions have been made between *imagination* and *creativity*, I haven't tried to pursue them in this book. For the purposes of writing and for reflecting on writing, I think of imagination as an intuitive mental capacity and creativity as the partly conscious process that can transform the operations of imagination into art.) Interestingly, the writing achievement levels defined by the National Assessment of Educational Progress (NAEP), the "Nation's Report Card," reserve the adjective *creative* for "Advanced" writing, while for "Proficient" writers the key adjective is *effective* and for "Basic" writers, *appropriate*. These distinctions seem to assume that we should expect creativity only of our very best writers, and that what is appropriate or effective writing need not possess any creativity—perhaps even that creativity isn't always appropriate? And as most teachers discover, what we expect of a student is all too often exactly what we get.

What is the opposite of creative writing? **Un**creative writing? You can't craft even a business memo or a set of instructions without first *imagining* your audience—*creating* in your mind a vision of their needs and assumptions; then you must listen, imaginatively, to your voice through their ears as you creatively weigh your words, and tighten and clarify, to persuade or inform those business colleagues. While few teenage writers thrill to the thought of creating memos or instructions, or the five-paragraph timed essay for that matter, they can develop good ears and sharp eyes for sentence structure, word choice, organization, even the semicolon, once their imaginations are fully engaged in shaping a piece they *want* to write. For many, that piece might be a story (a fictional narrative or a "true story"), a poem, or a short play—if their teacher offers them those choices.

In *Beyond Standards*, Carol Jago describes her initial skepticism when her ninth-grade son's teacher allowed him to write an adventure fantasy: "James needed practice with essays. What was the point of his writing a juvenile adventure story?" But gradually, she sees how completely invested he is in the project, what unusual care he takes with the writing and what risks he takes with sophisticated diction and tone: "To my mind the tale was obviously derivative of the fantasy books he had been reading, but to James it was utterly new, a story never told quite this way before. As he put words to paper I noticed that he cared a great deal about getting them down just right. He would bound out of his room asking, 'Now, what's the word for . . . ?' Going from a handwritten to a typed copy, he revised much more than I had seen him do for other assignments." She begins to speculate: "The occasional creative assignment might be of value to a novice writer, especially in terms of fostering a positive attitude toward writing." Her son's story has, moreover, satisfied California Writing Standards 2.1 a–d. Thinking about her own tightly packed sophomore and junior English curricula, in contrast to her twelfth-grade creative writing course, in which students "compose with delight," Jago concludes that "in the pursuit of intellectual rigor, I had denied students this pleasure for the last few years . . . . How much would it hurt to read one fewer book and instead write a story of their own?" (53–54)

Introduction, Draft B

Catching Tigers in Red Weather was inspired by a small student protest in my ninth-grade classroom—just one hand in the air, one kid asking, "Hey, Ms. Michaels, when do we get to write our own thing? I mean, free choice?"

"But you've had lots of choices already," I say indignantly. "I always give you more than one topic to choose from. You had three for your *Catcher in the Rye* response in Holden's voice, and four for the *"Master Harold" . . . and the boys* monologue, and you could write on anything at all for your "in the zone" description, and—"

"Yeah, but—Ms. Michaels, don't take this the wrong way or anything—those were all your choices. When do we get to write whatever we want?"

Heads are nodding vigorously. More hands are going up.

It's the day before Thanksgiving, almost time for the school assembly. I think fast and say, "How about the day we get back from vacation?"

"Yup. Sounds good," says Carlos.

And then I begin to wonder what I have let myself in for. Stories full of spaceships and weaponry, with interchangeable stick figures for characters? Sentimental poems full of clichés about broken relationships? Swords and sorcery. Vampire romance. Bad Writing. Is this going to be even remotely worthwhile? Pedagogically responsible? I know the research, and my past experience confirms it: guided choice good; free choice bad. I've been guiding their choices: a, b, or c. Now they want to invent their own alphabet? Besides, how can I hold conferences on so many different kinds of pieces? How will we assess them? Grade them? And how much time will this take away from what we're actually supposed to be doing next—Sophocles and more drill on avoiding comma splices? These aren't honors kids; we don't track. They're a mix, some coming up from our own heterogeneous eighth-grade classes and about one-third from various junior high schools around the area.

Cautiously I ask, "So Carlos, what do you want to write?"

He gets a dreamy look on his face. "Those old movies. Tough guy detective and blonde babes. And how stupid the way they talk always is. How they say the same clichés all the time. Film noir." He rolls the *r* dramatically.

Whispers run around the room. "What's film noir?" "He just said what it was, dummy."

"You mean you want to write a satire, Carlos? A parody?"

"Yup."

This definitely sounds like something Carlos could pull off, and it would be fun to read—which is a very big plus. I have to admit I'd never have thought to offer the students satire as an option. I once developed a senior-level satire course, but after teaching it for a couple of years I got frustrated with (1) having almost no girls sign up and (2) having to explain "what's so funny" all the time.

Now I'm wondering whether anyone else in the class besides Carlos has an idea—even a clue—about what they'd like to write.

"Let's open our writer's notebooks and take the next six minutes to brainstorm: What would you write if you could choose anything? Or what would you write about?"

Then I wonder, should we have made a list together first of genres—haiku, memoir, profiles, horror stories . . . ? But most of the class is already starting to write.

Six minutes later we go around the room hearing ideas.

Meade: "My dad and I saw this movie, where these two guys' job is to pull a lever if they're given a signal from headquarters, and it would fire these totally destructive weapons. And one of the guys is fine with that, but the other's starting to think he couldn't do it. But in the movie you don't get inside that second guy's head, so I'd like to write his story. I can talk about it with my dad over Thanksgiving."

Jacqui: "I'm going to write about my grandmother's funeral and how it was for me. I've been wanting to do this for months now, but there's been so much homework." (Ouch! I know just how she feels. Lines for a poem have been tugging at my sleeve for the past month.)

Alex: "Definitely a war story. That's my favorite. In Russia. This officer's beginning to have doubts about Communism, and he's going to get in trouble."

Maxime: "A story about Maxime the great—how he can do all these cool things and how wonderful he is."

Adam: "Something about running. I think it'll be a group of poems, but kind of like our 'in the zone' piece. Lots of images."

Sydney A.: "I don't know, let me think some more, oh, well, about auditioning for the eighth-grade musical last year. But I don't know how to write it."

Jacob: "I want to go on with the utopia I showed you in my notebook last conference. I've started adding appendixes about the countries outside the one I've made up, but I need to get back to the actual story and see what's going to happen to the main character."

Emma: "Maybe about ballet, how I love doing it. Or maybe . . . some poems. Love poems."

A.J.: "Tennis! Me and Federer."

Samantha: "Oh no, A.J., *I* want to write about tennis. You did that last time." (If Sami, who's always missing school for tournaments and is the county's number 1 player, can actually write about her love–hate relationship with the game, this would be a real breakthrough. She's one of the least experienced and weakest writers in the group.)

A few students have no ideas, so I urge them to think about it over vacation, but I'm amazed at the number who seem to know exactly what they want to write. Next day, somewhere between turkey and pies, I find myself thinking: You could build the whole year's curriculum around this project. But it's too late now. . . .

Commentary

These drafts, A and B, plus several more that ended up in the trash, I've written over the course of four days, sitting at the laptop or brooding in the kitchen as I fixed dinner or trying out individual sentences in my head during my afternoon run. I'm always worrying about first impressions. Will I sound like someone you'll want to stay with, for a few more pages at least? Who are you? Is anybody out there? Would a little dialogue reel you in? Or are you more of a "just give me the facts" sort? What do I want to do here—amuse you? Persuade you? Introduce myself? Establish a thesis? Inspire trust?

Yes.

So in this instance, I use both drafts. Two introductions to the introduction. A break with "the conventions." I want to include voice A, which uses "we" and "you" and offers a line of argument bolstered by research and by my experience as a writer. But I also want voice B, which will dominate in this book—a voice that makes its points through the presentation of classroom scenes in student voices, along with the recording, in first person, of my intentions, mistakes, revisions, and reflections as a teacher. As I drafted, trying out both voices, I found myself considering how I might offer them to my own students as samples of a writing process that goes beyond the traditional mantra of draft-revise-edit-publish, or even beyond what some writing textbooks call "global revision." Good writing is hard. But it's also play. I'm suddenly picturing our kindergartners outdoors at recess, playing hard. They're very reluctant to stop. The other day I saw a group of them fully engaged in covering a stuffed animal with petals they'd collected from a flowering bush: "We're having a funeral," one told me. I watched as wriggly five-year-olds formed a circle and stood quietly, no teacher present.

Writing can engage you more completely than you expected when you first sat down with a phrase or image or line of dialogue; you're surprised when you look up at the clock. Your creative imagination may have enticed you into trying on two different voices for your introduction, weighing their possibilities, and perhaps interweaving parts of both. Making a dialogue. Or a collage. Or just using both in their entirety. Risking hell for breaking the rules. Gradually, if you form the habit of reflection, you realize your best writing has involved constant creative choices as you listened to your thoughts, imagined various ways you could express them, and, at some stage, imagined how your readers would hear them. Good writing is by its nature *creative*.

Motivation: Writing as Art, No Matter the Genre or Purpose

All very well for admissions officers and test-makers and government committees to expect teenagers to respond "proficiently" in twenty-five minutes to a quotation they've never seen, for an audience of speed-reading adults counting up pieces of "supporting evidence." But just how should we, the writing teachers, motivate our students to learn the skills for this peculiar task? And is this what writing proficiency means?

From my own experience as a writer and teacher, I would say this: Arghhhh. No, seriously, we should help kids learn to enjoy writing for itself, to approach it as an art like music or Web design or moviemaking that engages their individual imaginations and lets them say something that matters to them, that has some of the power of their favorite books. (Even if those were their favorites back in fifth grade, after which some kids stopped reading.) Then they will learn, gradually, to care about everything that makes a writer proficient in any genre: word choice, sentence rhythms, organization, choice of details and evidence, pacing, research techniques, titles, beginnings and endings, the correct incorporation of quotations.

They will also gradually develop, with sufficient guidance and practice, the capacity to reflect on writing, their own and others'. As they reflect, they will make more discoveries, bring to a conscious level what they've been trying out by instinct, and begin to internalize criteria that will help them to make good creative choices in *all* the writing they do. Without my prescribing the five or six now-standard criteria for writing assessment, my ninth graders arrived at these criteria and more through consensus and in their own words, after discussing one another's drafts in relation to books we read and to older students' work. Given time to explore a range of genres through both reading and writing, and some carefully planned opportunities for choice, students can learn to "play hard" at writing and thereby become more proficient. More important, as they make choices, "make their mark" on the page, create pieces they're proud of, they discover that they care about reaching out to an audience, about reshaping their work with that imagined audience in mind. They begin to do what Katherine Paterson, author of *Bridge to Terabithia*, has said is our fundamental task as human beings—exercising our imaginations in order to seek connection with others. She goes on to conclude, "It follows then, that the basic task of education is the care and feeding of the imagination" (60). Success at this "basic" task is impossible to measure and doesn't appear in any published list of "standards" that I've seen, but it's worth considering.

When Brent Staples, writing in the *New York Times,* exhorts schools to produce the writers "required by the new economy," trained to write "clear, concise communication, which all business people want to read" (qtd. in Slouka 34), I find myself thinking, Okay, clarity and concision are fine, but as a teacher of the art and craft of writing, I'd like to help produce not only future employees in the global economy but also imaginative friends, siblings, lovers, neighbors, grown sons and daughters, and parents of imaginative teenagers. Given this task, how many scripted lessons, usage drills, and practice tests have we time for?

The Free-Choice Writing Project

So the summer after we had muddled our way, at Carlos's behest, through the free-choice writing project, I sat in an empty classroom with a stack of writing folders and took stock. Initially, I'd been amazed that so many of these students knew what they wanted to write. A few changed their minds partway into the project, and a few needed me to talk them through some options. But I think we'd done enough varied writing assignments in the fall and shared our work with enough enthusiasm that by Thanksgiving the confidence and sense of ownership were there. Kids seemed comfortable with one another and eager to write something for the class to read. But for two or three weeks during the project, I'd had to watch for teachable moments in which to improvise mini-lessons. It seemed as though every day I was searching for strategies that might work across genres: the concept of pacing, for instance, of where the story or profile or poem or parody needed to be speeded up with summarizing, or where a moment needed to be slowed down, "cracked open," as Ralph Fletcher says, with details. It felt like I was continually holding conferences, sometimes with the story group or the nonfiction group, sometimes with one individual, in class and out of class, face-to-face and online. I sensed I was learning, along with my students, but I didn't have time to figure out exactly *what*. Finally, the day before winter break, I handed out the class anthology and we held a celebratory read-aloud.

Almost every student said in his or her assessment the following June that this was the best experience they'd had all year. They ranked it right up there with learning fight techniques from visiting actors and staging the brawl in *Othello*. Many of them commented that having a teacher take their choices seriously enough to give three weeks to the writing project was part of what made it "awesome." One boy said his previous teacher had assigned a short story to be written in only one night, so he'd never gotten to figure out an ending. I was surprised he'd even gotten that far, but I sympathized with his teacher's desire to cram in one more genre. My student said it seemed as though his eighth grade had spent all year writing essays arguing for and against school uniforms.

Most of the students said they'd worked harder on this piece than they'd ever worked before in English class—that making it good really mattered because it was their own and because they wanted their friends to like it. I remembered that in most cases their revisions had been "global," not just a matter of correcting some misplaced commas. But I also remembered how hard it was for them to connect their free-choice writing with the writing they'd done earlier that year—to build on their past experience. My fault:

whatever scaffolding they'd had was accidental, assignments created in response to the books we were reading—a dialogue between two characters, a page written in Holden Caulfield's voice, an informal response to a few poems, a paragraph interpreting the ending of Fugard's play *"Master Harold" . . . and the boys.* Good assignments, but maybe I'd focused on them too much as *reading* responses and not enough as lessons in the craft of *writing.*

As I returned to the possibility of building an entire course around this project, I tried the idea out on some colleagues. "Why not give them more time to learn skills, and move the free choice up to June? It could be your final exam," my department chair suggested. But I already had in place a final exam that served as a good culmination of the full year's work. I liked the idea of making the free-choice writing project be a climax to the first half of the year—something exciting to look forward to and to learn from afterward.

Scheduling the project that early meant I would have to plan my opening units very carefully. I'd need to make a more conscious effort to build up the students' writing repertoire of genres and skills—and heighten their awareness of what they were learning—so that they'd be prepared to handle whatever type of piece they chose. This meant more reflection on their writing, from them and from me. Maybe it meant fewer discussions of the literature. (Could I cut out one book? I'd have to ask the English grade 9 teaching team.) I would try to create more of a studio atmosphere, as Donald Graves recommended so many years ago—make more class time available for actually drafting and responding to one another's drafts and for learning to read as writers—using the class texts and one another's writing as models. The literature would have to become more than just the illustration of English grade 9's journey theme. I would share my own writing more often in rough draft, let students watch me struggle with choices and surprises along the way, let them see me cross out, rethink. Graves reassures us: "Teachers don't have to be expert writers to 'write' with the children. In fact, there may be an advantage in growing with them, learning together as both seek to find meaning in writing" (43).

I couldn't change the theme or texts for grade 9 English—"the personal journey," as viewed through two novels, three plays, a month of poetry, and some contemporary essays; and anyway, the theme felt right for ninth graders, kids who are so aware of being in a new place, making a new start. It offered good opportunities for writing in different genres. I liked the Essential

Questions our teaching team had created, too: How do we get to know one another on our journeys? How do we get beyond first impressions, first assumptions? When do you think the rights of the individual should take precedence over those of society or over the law—if ever? What beliefs or rights would you risk standing up for, and what might these risks entail? How does your private self differ from your public self? To what extent do you feel your sense of who you are is changing? How much is it shaped by your age, race, gender, class, religion, sexual orientation? By family and environment? What are your views on fate versus free will? What are your sources of power? Of courage? In what ways have fear, jealousy, love shaped your life? Consider the archetypal heroic journey in relation to your own: Who and what have been your mentors, monsters? Any quests? What thresholds have you crossed so far?

I liked this material. It all related to the personal journey of becoming a writer, of exploring one's voice through making choices. I just had to refocus to make the texts and questions serve our writing needs more fully. Oh dear, and it was already mid-August!

A Description of Catching Tigers

Catching Tigers in Red Weather describes the subsequent writing curriculum that I designed for the first half of the year, from September to late December, and how my ninth graders and I carried it out. I take my title from Wallace Stevens's "Disillusionment of Ten o'Clock," because the poem celebrates color, risk, imagination, and originality and, I think, implies that these qualities may be found in unexpected places. A student who's never written an essay he liked may suddenly catch fire when he discovers a poem by Mark Doty that speaks to him; he may even go on to create a vivid, authentic poem of his own, just as Stevens's "old sailor, / Drunk and asleep in his boots / Catches Tigers / In red weather." All the conventional people asleep in their houses and wearing white night-gowns "are not going / To dream of baboons and periwinkles," let alone of catching tigers. The poem calls up old sailor wisdom: "Red sky at night, sailor's delight. Red sky at morning, sailors take warning." All of us—teachers and students—who care about the adventure of writing, or are learning to care, find ourselves sooner or later encountering both danger and delight as we sail off to catch our tiger. We learn that sometimes we must trust intuition, or the unconscious, or plain old luck and let the conventional logic that makes outlines and follows rules go to sleep for a bit. We discover the power of the unexpected—the night-gowns that are "purple with green rings."

Catching Tigers demonstrates ways to give *all* students experience in creative writing within the context of a standard literature curriculum (my class is not an honors group) and how those genres that they study as texts but are rarely taught to write—in particular, poetry and the fictional and personal narrative—give them access to strategies that can enliven all their writing, including the analytical essay, with its emphasis on argument and persuasion. I try to bring this process to life for you through classroom scenes so that you can hear actual discussions and conferences; watch how theater games, debates, and music prepare these varied learners to write; observe students and teacher creating assessment criteria together for specific writing assignments; visit the Writing Center; and see student pieces take shape. Important parts of this weave are the voices of writers and teachers I've learned from, along with my own reflections and lesson planning process as I try to break down the traditional barriers between creative and academic writing, between one genre and another, and search for their commonalities. Throughout, I'm trying to help my writers make connections as they experiment with various genres—to discover, for example, how imagining and creating a fictional character's voice relates to envisioning and fulfilling a reading audience's needs. Both require empathy, not just specific writing skills. Both necessitate the shaping of language—imagery, sentence structure, sound patterns, paragraph coherence, line breaks, the subordination of evidence to idea or argument. They involve the workings of both reason and imagination, of heart, body, and mind.

It's important to me that *Catching Tigers* proceed by "showing" as much as by "telling." When, as a young teacher in the 1970s, I discovered the firsthand accounts by visiting writers in the New York City schools (Kenneth Koch, Philip Lopate, etc.), I thought, "Oh, that's what a class of student writers sounds like when it catches fire." Much later, I read poet Georgia Heard's *For the Good of the Earth and Sun* and listened hard to the students she wrote about: "By reading it out loud, you feel the meaning of the poem," a third grader tells her (7). I listened to Heard reflecting on a particular lesson she was in the midst of teaching: "It always moves me when kids leave the stereotype of what they've been taught about poetry and come up with their own definitions. '*Songs with no music,*' I say. 'That sounds like a great way to describe a poem.' I let that one sink into me" (15). And just recently, I listened to Jeffrey Golub in *Making Learning Happen* as he re-created "one of those messy lesson-planning efforts" to show us "a more realistic picture of how lesson-planning often proceeds" when you "can't provide ready answers to the four basic lesson-planning questions" (103). I don't want books that just tell me what to do, even when the ideas sound good or are grounded in the latest pedagogy; I want to see those ideas taking shape and being tried out in real classrooms.

So while my specific texts, assignments, and assessment criteria are all present, *Catching Tigers* is designed as a series of invitations, not a set of directives. Readers can decide which invitations to accept by seeing and hearing the preparation and process for each writing assignment. To emphasize the value of following the stream of classroom talk and activities, I've used headings to focus on the key ideas they illustrate; I realize that most of us are reading—dancing, juggling—as fast as we can. Where my reflections look back to assess how far the class has come and then look ahead to figure out where we should go next, I head these passages "So Far/What Next?" For each writing assignment, I describe:

1. My rationale for the assignment—in particular, what new choices it offers the students, why I position it at this point in the course, and what strategies and skills it is intended to teach

2. The related class texts, the role of writer's notebook, class discussion, use of models, the drafting process, mini-lessons, the creating of assessment criteria by students and teacher, peer response or student–teacher conferences or conferences with an older writing mentor, revision, and sometimes "publication" (a reading, a performance, a class collection)

The book includes samples of students' work in various stages, as well as some of their self-assessments and reflections. I also explain and demonstrate the workings of our school's student-staffed Writing Center. In the epilogue, I include the texts of the second part of the year and several of the main writing assignments, including the Shakespeare essay (on *Othello*) and the final exam project. I also discuss how my students' writing discoveries and skills measure up against the Common Core State Standards for writing.

Because I believe in the importance of teachers writing alongside their students and sometimes sharing their drafts or processes, several chapters begin with some writing of my own that relates to that chapter's focus—a poem and the journal entry from which it grew, an email exchange, an assignment I tested out before giving it to my class—along with a commentary about what writing this piece teaches me that I can share with my students. Several chapters begin with work by a student and one with a journal entry by playwright Athol Fugard.

Some Recommendations

I know that many of us are hesitant to teach the writing of stories and poetry, perhaps because we've never written in these genres ourselves, or we're not sure how to assess them. As a poet, I'm still feeling my way with fiction, but I'm finding it an exciting adventure, and I can recommend some books that have helped me.

For those of you who teach in a particularly prescriptive school district, Rebecca Sipe's book *Adolescent Literacy at Risk? The Impact of Standards* offers helpful descriptions of ways that innovative teachers have worked and can work together within a school to develop curricula that are true to best practices while working within a standards-based framework. Carol Jago's *Cohesive Writing* is another useful book in its illustration of how preparation for high-stakes testing and showing teenagers how writing can be a way to learn about themselves need not be mutually exclusive agendas.

Catching Tigers offers simply one teacher's design, one individual effort to move high school writers toward and beyond proficiency by appealing to their creativity and their growing desire for independence. It's an effort that grows out of what I know many of us are struggling to do, and I know this from listening to teachers' voices online, in books, and at conferences: to teach not just the test, the skills, or even the standards, but the student. The kid who wants to write a parody of a movie, a song lyric for his band, a piece about being at her grandmother's funeral, a rave review of vampire books, a poem about a friend killed in a car crash, a description of a Civil War battle, a fantasy with talking animals—or the kid who doesn't know what he wants to write and just needs some help in finding out. I hope in this book you will find ideas you can adapt to your own classes, ideas that will help you continue our struggle to care for and feed the imagination as we guide students to write—not just proficiently but creatively.

Chapter 2

Building a Community of Writers

Part One—Laying Foundations
Starting the Ninth-Grade Journey

When I left high school behind and headed off to college, I was scared but exultant. "I can make a whole new start here. Not a single person knows me. I won't be the teacher's daughter, shy and studious, in love with classical music, embarrassed to dance the Twist. Nobody will know I've never had a drink, never been kissed . . . never eaten pizza." I hugged Dad goodbye, leaving a smear of dark red lipstick on his white shirt (no more Tangee Natural for me!) and imagined a total transformation. Within a month, I knew it hadn't worked when my first date—now husband of many years—told me how one guy in his dorm said, "Oh, you're going out with her? The one who always looks like she's walking on eggs?"

As I watch my ninth graders come into class on the first day of school, I suspect a lot of them, too, are looking to reinvent themselves. One-third of these kids are "new." They don't know anyone. Since we're a K–12 school, the rest of the students have come up from our junior high—a few, the "lifers," even from junior kindergarten. They know the building and the school culture. But for everyone here, high school is a new deal.

The theme of our school's grade 9 English curriculum is the journey, archetypal and personal—the developing, expressing, questioning, concealing, and testing of identity. From past experience, I know that one particular aspect of the journey will be a constant in our classroom: how we learn to know and communicate with others. And how, partly through this process, we come to know ourselves. But at the start of the year, ninth graders tend to be more interested in taking stock of their peers than in doing much self-analysis—or textual analysis, for that matter. So I want their first major writing project to be a profile of a partner, a short piece that grows out of conversations and emails with a classmate. I want them all to learn how to question, how to show interest, how to imagine. "You sound like you love being the youngest in your family. Are there, um, any down sides? Really? Don't your older brothers make fun of you a lot? Mine do . . . and I'm always the last one to get to do stuff." "Your dad's a teacher here? So what's that like? Yeah, not much privacy? So he wants to choose your friends for you? What do you do about that?" I want them to pay attention to voice, how it characterizes a person; how a quotation, well chosen and effectively used, can convey more than factual information, can be full of attitude. Figuring out ways to present their partner to us on paper through informing, quoting, and reflecting will help them later to understand various fictional characters, even to create some. It may also help them reflect on how, consciously and unconsciously, they present themselves to others.

I'll ask the students for a single "beefy" paragraph, roughly one typed page, so that they can start working right away on the challenge of synthesizing their information around a single topic, viewing it through a single lens. Their tendency will be to create three to five dinky paragraphs, stopping and starting them rather randomly and perhaps repeating material to link one to another; but instead, I want them to see how richly developed a single paragraph can be, especially when it starts with a strong hook and moves, following some clearly marked order, to a reflective conclusion. Many of my students will not have encountered a paragraph this long, let alone written one. They'll gradually discover the need for clear transitions within the paragraph, between its individual sentences. Later we can explore the power and rhythm of other unfamiliar possibilities—the single-sentence paragraph, the poem with stanzas of varying lengths. While I want them to build on what they already know and to feel confident, I also want them to question the norm, or what they assume to be the norm, both in writing and in relating to their peers. Ursula Le Guin, in her wonderful little book on writing, *Steering the Craft*, has a useful "opinion piece on paragraphing," which I may read from in class when we start structuring our profiles:

> I have found in several how-to-write books statements such as, "Your novel should begin with a one-sentence paragraph," "No paragraph in a story should contain more than four sentences," and so on. Rubbish! Such "rules" originated in periodicals printed in columns—newspapers, pulp magazines, *The New Yorker*—which really do have to break the tight grey density of the print with frequent indents, large initial caps, and line breaks. . . . But you don't have to do it to your own prose. "Rules" about keeping sentences and paragraphs short are mechanical spin-offs from journalism and a highly artificial school of action writing. If you obey them, you'll probably sound like second-class Hemingway. (50)

Another reason to start the year with a profile: it's a new genre for most ninth graders. Although they may think of it at first as a kind of report, the term *profile* makes them feel quite adult, or at least really in high school. Many will worry that they won't be able to extract enough material from the interview, and most will have trouble organizing it into a cohesive, one-page article, but they'll be engaged by the challenge. The project will also give me a chance to introduce them to our high school newspaper, which is full of interviews at this time of year, and to some of the staff; it's important for ninth graders to meet older students who take writing seriously. These juniors and seniors, along with the Writing Center mentors and the literary magazine staff, are all a part of our writing community. So are those faculty members who write. Our religion and philosophy teacher and our diversity coordinator both write poetry; so do three members of my own department. Later in the year, I'll be bringing some of them into class.

Another part of our community will be the great writing teachers whose wisdom we'll be sharing, as we move from one genre to the next: Donald Murray, Tom Romano, Georgia Heard, Ralph Fletcher, Ursula Le Guin, Anne Lamott, Naomi Shihab Nye, Annie Dillard, William Zinsser.

Preliminaries to the Interview

Before conducting interviews, the students need to learn how to listen and to speak to one another, look their peers in the eye, read gestures and facial expression (those clues that may be overlooked by an online generation), and exhibit some interest in what others say about themselves. Before they write a profile, I want them to become more aware of how to move beyond hearsay and first impressions, to think about how you start getting to know another person firsthand and how you allow, even help, that person to know you. There are plenty of getting-acquainted and community-building games to play. I like those described by Jeffrey Golub in *Making Learning Happen* —scavenger hunt, simultaneous interviews, simultaneous monologues, "the king and his servants," writer's profile, "tell us about . . ."—because they engage everyone immediately in speaking and listening, even the shy or the skeptical. Bruce Pirie's *Teenage Boys and High School English* also offers some thoughtful exercises in listening and speaking, valuable for both genders, which start by asking students to write a brief recollection of a time when they felt they weren't being listened to—how they knew, how it made them feel, what they did. This quickwrite leads easily to discussion of some roadblocks to real listening and can move on into work with "subtext," "thought balloons," and "decoding"—which would be useful for my students' discussions of Holden Caulfield later in the fall and their writing in Holden's voice. As Pirie points out to those of us who worry that we "don't have time to add in a whole unit on group processes," these activities needn't constitute a separate unit. "Many works of literature already deal with communication problems and the failures of community, and it makes sense to address those concerns in ways that connect with our own relationships." He cites *Lord of the Flies, A Separate Peace, Animal Farm, Black Boy, Ordinary People,* and *One Flew Over the Cuckoo's Nest* (118). I've created two games, "eye-to-eye" and "pebble/marble" (see Michaels, *Dancing with Words*), which I'll play with the ninth graders during our first two classes, before we begin interviews and profiles.

Eye-to-Eye

On this first day, I like to introduce the skill of listening to one another with the close *looking* at one another. I also want to pose a problem that will move students around the room and encourage them to work together. So after introducing myself, I ask the students to see how fast they can arrange themselves into a standing circle according to eye color; no verbal communication is allowed, but gestures are fine. I ask them to observe everyone's eyes closely so that in the circle we'll end up with the dark browns shading down to the light browns, etc. Once the circle's made, I walk around inside it, quietly looking into eyes and starting to get to know these kids. I ask them to steer me to the right spot, somewhere among the blues. There's a little giggling as students stare into my eyes. Then we sit down on the floor in our circle, and we read aloud a poem by Naomi Shihab Nye, "Eye-to-Eye," each of us reading a line.

Eye-to-Eye

Please forgive this interruption.
I am forging a career,
A delicate enterprise
of eyes. Yours included.
We will meet at the corner,
you with your sack lunch,
me with my guitar.
We will be wearing our famous street faces,
anonymous as trees.
Suddenly you will see me,
you will blink, hesitant,
then realize I have not looked away.
For one brave second
we will stare
openly
from borderless skins.
This is my salary.
There are no days off.

We run through the poem several times till we can read smoothly, expressively, and with eye contact. I tell them that former Poet Laureate Robert Hass says when you read a poem aloud, you're taking the poet's breath—the rhythm of flow, stop, start—onto your own breath. "That's kind of spooky and powerful to think about, isn't it? Somebody else's breathing coming alive again inside you?" And finally, we do some exploratory writing to discover our individual thoughts about the poem, especially what it implies about communication. I suggest they also consider how this writing might connect with our eye-to-eye game and our collaborative reading aloud. I want students to experience how writing can help them think and make discoveries. And I want them to test Nye's writing and thinking against their own experiences. Both of these processes can help them conduct their interviews and draft the profiles.

Tonight, in addition to continuing their exploratory writing, the ninth graders will fill out an information sheet on themselves that I'll staple to their pages in my grade book, as well as a summer reading card listing any books, magazines, and newspapers they read or reread; any art exhibits, concerts, plays, or "especially memorable" movies they saw; a favorite book from childhood; and a favorite book from the past couple of years. The cards sit in a basket on my desk, so we can discuss them in conferences and students can add new items. Some of my colleagues have students keep their records online. Our department requires independent reading—at least two books a term—and builds in five or ten minutes at the start of class for it. I read along with the students, though I also take time to run an eye around the room to keep tabs on who is reading what, who's forgotten to bring a book, who's making very slow progress, and who might need a different book.

Pebble/Marble

The next day I've slotted for the pebble/marble game, another chance for us all to get better acquainted. But it's also a lesson in the power of specificity. We sit in a floor circle, again by eye color so that friends won't cluster and unintentionally create a ghetto of new kids. I lead the class in a short breathing exercise with their eyes closed, to get them quiet inside. Then, keeping their eyes closed, each student picks a pebble and a marble by feel out of a box I pass around. I ask them to hold one in each hand, feel the differences in shape, size, and texture; then to think about one worry and one hope for the year that they can tell us about when it's their turn to say their name and put their pebble and marble in the middle of the circle. (I don't allow "bad grades" as a pebble; if I don't remember to ban grades, half the class mentions them and we learn nothing new about one another.) As we go around, I push for specifics: is it more interesting to know that someone's looking forward to auditioning for the fall play, or to also learn a bit about the *why*, the back story? This, I point out, is a principle that will hold true for writing as well as speaking—the value of the specific, the significant details that individualize a person or place or thing, that help us know who you are. "As you listen to your classmates' voices, think about what it will feel like to be part of this group. Whose hopes or worries do you find it easiest to relate to? Whose surprise you? Whose make you want to hear more?"

I also point out that we can do various kinds of sharing, depending on our comfort level with the group: "I've been teaching so long, and meeting so many new students over the years, that I'm pretty comfortable opening up right away with some fairly heavy stuff, but you don't have to." I emphasize that it's going to be important, all year, to respect each person's views and make class a safe place for sharing things—our writing, our ideas about books and life. Maybe some of these things will be hard to talk about. I suggest that "safe" means recognizing when something spoken or written should not go beyond this classroom. I also explain, right here at the outset, that if I hear or read anything that suggests someone is a danger to themselves or to others, I can't, legally, keep it confidential—and that I wouldn't want to.

"All right, everybody ready? Open your eyes."

During the game, I have to keep asking for more detail and reminding students to speak up, to make eye contact—risk eye-to-eye—and to be fully present as listeners. What does that mean, "fully present as listeners?" In *Letters to a Young Artist*, the playwright, actor, and teacher Anna Deavere Smith writes,

> I do think we need to create our classroom as an oasis where different kinds of exploration and creation can happen, where the boundaries are different from what they are in everyday life. . . . I strive to be the best audience a student can have, and everyone in the class must also strive to be so. You should make note on the first day of who is, and who is not, a good audience . . . and viewer. . . . Some people will sit in a very disinterested way. In the course of time, I actively try to change those people. Body language matters. (103)

Smith is talking about theater class, but ours too needs to become a performance space. We pause to talk about ways someone can show he or she is listening. I watch interactions, because in a few days I'll be pairing students up for interviews. I listen hard for clues to who these strangers are and for hints about what topics they may want to write about during the year, what Donald Graves calls their "territories of interest."

I always go first with marble and pebble. For the past twelve years, I've used my recurrent ovarian cancer as my pebble, partly to open the way for anyone who wants to risk a heavy topic of their own and partly to explain that the cancer's occurred five times now, about every two years, and that when it does I'm usually away a month after surgery and then back in school during the months of chemotherapy. I want to forestall the gossip they'll hear from older students and the insecurity they may feel about a teacher who, it might seem to them, could disappear at any time. I also know the odds are that at least one student in this circle is dealing with a family member's cancer, and that it may help to see someone who's survived for so long. Over the past twelve years, I can remember at least four students who were cancer patients themselves. "If anyone in here should want to talk with me about cancer, maybe because you're worried about someone who has it, I'm available any time," I add. My marble usually has something to do with poetry—a reading I'm going to, a collection I'm working on, a poet I've just discovered in a magazine.

Once I've finished, I get up and move around the outside of the circle to stand behind whoever's speaking, so that person won't be tempted to speak to me rather than to the class. (In desperation, I once tried hiding behind my big desk, but students started addressing themselves to the desk.) "You could start by making eye contact with someone you know, someone who might smile back at you. This is what I do when I'm giving a poetry reading. Then get braver and start looking around the room. Talk to all of us. And listeners, look at the speaker. Send out some waves, some good vibrations of interest. Don't get preoccupied with what you'll say when it's your turn."

When the pile of pebbles and marbles is complete, I remind everyone that, in a limited way, this heap of rock says who we are as a group, the things we have in common, some things that make each of us unique. This year, two students are hopeful—or worried—about the presidential election; quite a few are already missing friends from their former schools or kids from our junior high who've moved away; one says she hopes the cliques from last year will break up this year, "now that we're in high school and more mature"; many are hoping to make new friends; at least four have grandparents or other family members who are seriously ill; an anxious baseball player is still on crutches from last spring's injuries; one boy's father is in Iraq; a girl is worrying about a friend with an eating disorder. I ask everyone to think about how fears and hopes are important parts of who we are—possible motives for what we do, especially choices we make, both good and bad. I tell them this is true for fictional characters, too—ones they read about and ones they might invent in their writing.

So Far/What Next?

In these first two classes together, students have had to pay attention to the people around them—a good habit for writers to develop—by looking one another in the eye and using gestures to solve a problem; by listening to one another's voices and supporting that listening with eye contact; and by considering how best to communicate aloud, using voices and eyes to share personal feelings and to create a collaborative reading of a poem. They've been encouraged to respect their own and each other's hopes and worries about the coming year, not only as a means of getting to know their peers but also as an opportunity for self-reflection and (perhaps risky) self-expression. All these processes help lay the foundations for a writing community.

Students have experienced the process of quickwriting to a prompt, an ungraded opportunity to use writing as free-form inquiry into a poem and its relation to their lives. (They may or may not have noticed that the prompt was very broad and didn't ask them to say "what the poem means.") They've seen how far they could get with this writing in class and where they could take it in ten more minutes at home; maybe some have become aware of which writing venue works best for them and of what's gained by letting a piece set and returning to it later. I've had my first opportunity to watch each of them write, to hear each of them speak to the group, and to observe their body language as speakers and listeners. And, through their information sheets, I'm starting to learn a little about their interests and reading preferences.

I hope I've prepared them well for two community-building writing assignments—the interview/profile and, following that, a short personal narrative about "a time when you were in the zone." These pieces will introduce a mix of genres and a variety of skills, as well as the experiences of writing mentor visits, class creation of evaluation criteria, mini-lessons, some use of the online class conference, peer editing, teacher conferences, and revision.

All of this, I've decided, will occur before we begin reading the works in the curriculum, though we're already exploring the theme of the personal journey that unites our reading and writing for the year. It feels important to establish these students as *writers*—as kids who see themselves as writers—before I bring in such big guns as J. D. Salinger, Mark Doty, Athol Fugard, E. E. Cummings. Kids can't "read as writers" until they've started to *feel* like writers.

Part Two—Writing the Profile

Nick in the Spotlight, a Profile by Judy Michaels

"I thought I was really dancing. But I was only moving around. What did I know? I was only five. My parents had just taken me to see *The Lion King*." And ever since that fateful trip, Nick's been dancing—and singing and acting. Now, at fourteen, he can look back on a series of professional credits: In fifth grade, part of a child army in a modern version of *Hamlet*—earnings, $100; then for three straight years, a role in McCarter Theater's *A Christmas Carol,* initially as part of the children's ensemble but eventually as Peter Cratchitt, Tiny Tim's younger brother. He earned less for that stint than for *Hamlet*, but he got to do more acting, more work. Listen to Nick talk about his love for theater and you realize very quickly that the pay doesn't matter—it's the passion. "I can express my feelings through theater. It's a great way to open up to people and let them know who I am and what my passion is," he says. Acting, whether in straight drama or in musicals, energizes him—though after a few minutes in conversation with Nick, it's impossible to imagine him without energy. But, he explains, he's always very calm right before he goes on stage, in order to be fully aware when he actually has to act. "With live theater you always have to be aware. And you need a quick mind. . . .You're in another world, relating to your character." I wondered whether these qualities were present in other areas of his life. Nick thought for a minute and then described a summer trip where he spent some time just watching the ocean—the fish, the different shades of the water. "Acting makes me notice things I wouldn't see otherwise," he said. "I was quiet for so long, my mom was worried!" Does he hope for a career in theater? Yes, but also in architecture, a combination he realizes might be hard to pull off. Next year he'll take architecture, but for now, having already enjoyed the drama elective in eighth grade, he's chosen a course in Advanced Acting, where he'll read a play each week and get a lot of experience in partnering. Recently he went into New York for a workshop in improvisation and expects to take more such workshops in the city. He's just read the school fall play, Arthur Miller's *The Crucible*, and is eager to audition: "Eighteen good roles. I could be happy with any of them." And then in the winter he'll try out for the musical. I'd like to have seen Nick in last year's eighth-grade show, *Damn Yankees*, where he got to sing and dance as a member of the baseball team. Or maybe even better to have seen him in the fourth-grade operetta, *Into the Woods*, as a dancing bear. So far it's been a rich and varied career.

Commentary

I drafted this profile of Nick after reading his brief paragraph on how much
he loves theater and having a fifteen-minute interview with him. Aside
from the fact that I *had* to partner someone for the profile because the
numbers were uneven, I wanted to do the assignment along with the class.
My participation might help validate it for them and would enable me to
recognize potential problems I could help them solve as we worked together. Nick chose a fine "window" or "lens" through which we—the class and
I—could view him. He was an easy subject, chatty and enthusiastic, though
not always listening very carefully to my questions so that I had to ask a
lot of them twice to find out what I wanted to know. I think he assumed he
knew what I was going to ask—a problem that was to continue all year in
our writing conferences together. Since other interviews were going on all
around us, I sometimes interrupted to share with the other pairs a problem
or possibility I'd just noticed in my work with Nick. "Make sure, folks, that if
you don't get all that you hoped in answer to a question, you rephrase it or
ask a follow-up question. And be flexible, because your partner may bring
up some aspect you didn't really think to ask about that may turn out to be
useful material. I'm finding this out as I talk with Nick."

Later in the process, when the class began looking at profiles by former
students and interviews in the school newspaper, I posted my profile on
Nick to our online class conference and, with his permission, the initial
statement he'd given me on acting, so that students could see what new
information I'd gotten from interviewing him and how I was incorporating
Nick's voice through quotations. I never offer my work as the sole model for
a particular assignment, as if there were one "right" way to do it, but it helps
students in mid-draft to see my process, especially if we analyze it together.

Here is the initial statement Nick gave me, on which I based my interview questions:

> Acting has always been a huge part of my life. From when I was very
> little and loved to sing, act and dance, to when I was in my first musical.
> Acting has always influenced me to be who I am and stand out. I also can
> express my feelings, thoughts, and ideas through acting. It's always been
> such a great experience to get up on stage with spotlights on you and sing
> or dance or act for an audience. I am always calm right before or after I
> act during a scene because it makes me energized and aware in the scene

when I act. And with live theater you always have to be aware. I chose this
item because it really shows what I love to do and tells a lot about me. It
is also a great way to open up to people and let them know who I am and
what my passion is.

Choosing a Lens

Over the weekend, I'm busy pairing up students for the profile project. I've
read the questionnaires they filled out, their quickwrites on Naomi Shihab
Nye's "Eye-to-Eye," and their summer reading cards. I'm trying to put kids
together who share an interest, but most of all I want to match new students
with old. I want to avoid pairing two kids who have been good friends for
years and know all there is to know about each other.

On Monday I explain that since so much of ninth grade, especially at the
outset, is about getting to know people—classmates, teachers, the older students—we're going to make interviews and profiles our first writing project.
I write the word *profile* on mural paper I've taped to the wall.

"How many different meanings can you think of for this word? Remember, writing is often a way to help us think, to discover what we know that
maybe we weren't aware we knew. So take a couple of minutes now to write
down whatever this word brings up for you. What images, pictures, associations come to mind? What ideas?" I don't ask them to write definitions. That
sounds so schoolish and dry. We can always go to dictionaries later. When
possible, I want the exploration of language to originate in the students' own
minds.

The students bring up racial profiling—"like, the police stop more black
drivers, just because of their skin color." They mention looking at someone
"in profile," drawing a profile of a face. And someone important "having a
high profile." "Or it can mean a biography, right?" asks Jess. I write all this
up on the wall, then ask if they see anything these different meanings have
in common. This is harder—analysis, comparison, synthesis. But finally
Peter says, "I guess they're all about a partial view. Like, just an outline, or
one side of someone. That is, if the biography is short and just goes for one
angle on a person."

"Do you see how Peter got that?" Heads nod. "I noticed you're all using
profile, or *profiling*, as a noun, a thing. But it can also be a verb. You can
profile someone—which is what we'll be doing for this writing project.
You're going to work in pairs to write a profile of your partner for the rest

of us—not a long biography and not a multiparagraph essay but a one-page, richly developed, double-spaced paragraph that will show us a particular aspect of this person. One angle. If we publish all these profiles together in a class collection, it'll be like the heap of hopes and worries we had on the floor last week—the pebbles and marbles—another view of who we are."

I ask students to look around the room and see which people they don't know yet. "Now suppose you wanted one of these people to start getting to know *you*: what might be an interesting aspect of your life that would shed some light on who you are? Your partner will need help from you to find a topic on which to focus the interview questions and the profile." I ask them to make a list of possibilities, maybe three or four potentially rich topics or lenses. "No, you won't find out who your partner is till tomorrow."

I walk around. Students seem engaged, thoughtful. I make my own list. Then we share. I ask them to listen especially carefully to the people they know best and see whether those lists sound like good choices. Matt tells Brooks, "Yeah, baseball, it's gotta be baseball!" Sydney exclaims, "Connor, I didn't know you went to South Africa this summer. That's so amazing. You should definitely use that." We're learning some of our peers' "territories of knowledge," and I'm realizing once again the importance of Donald Graves's point about this being one of the critical elements for the studio atmosphere: "The teacher is not some kind of holy figure dispensing topical grace. . . . The best confirmation comes from children who note what other children know" (23).

But I can help students think a little further—discover more of their territories. I hand out tonight's assignment (see Figure 2.1). When I'd first decided to try interviews, I thought I could just pair up students and then let them write questions to ask their partners and use the answers to introduce their partners to us. I had nothing more complicated in mind. Then I discovered Linda Rief's fine interview exercise in *Seeking Diversity* and tried that, but it took my students a long time to ask five broad questions, push for more detailed answers, ask five more questions on the most promising of their topics, and arrive at a good focus for the piece. So I built in the step of having the interviewees themselves select and write about three possible lenses. Gradually, what I'd seen as a brief community-building exercise stretched into several weeks and became the profile assignment. I suspected that filling out and posting online my own profile topics would help clarify the directions, inspire timid students, and push the procrastinators a little. It would also let the class get to know me a little better.

To help your partner get to know you better in your interview, fill in the three items below with brief descriptions (on separate paper):

1. A photo of you with at least one family member—this photo means something to you, for whatever reasons, and talking about it would shed light on you

2. An activity you love, or an event you loved, that sheds light on you (this might be from the list you made in class)

3. A specific memory that involves or evokes strong feelings of sadness or happiness for you and talking about it would shed light on you

Now choose whichever ONE of these three items you think sheds the most light on who you are, and spend around 30 minutes thinking, remembering, writing.* You may freewrite as images and ideas occur to you, or tell a story, or write a page of strong, detailed notes that will help you talk about this with your interview partner in class tomorrow. Draw on several of the five senses (taste, touch, smell, hearing, sight) to write on <u>EACH</u> of the following aspects of whichever one item you've chosen.

a. The setting (weather? season? time of day/night? smells in the air? sounds? etc.)

b. The action/situation (were others involved? who or what was moving/still? what colors did you notice? did the pace of the action/situation shift? which senses became more acute at particular moments?)

c. The mood or feeling involved (try to locate your feelings in your body: how did your stomach feel? your palms? the back of your neck? your knees? etc.)

d. Why you chose this item out of the three

e. What you feel it shows about you

*If you choose to use the photograph, try to bring it to class with you.

FIGURE 2.1. PROFILE QUESTIONNAIRE—40 MINUTES.

Hi, folks. Here's the way I did the profile prep homework for tomorrow. I probably can write faster than most of you, so I gave myself 30 minutes instead of 40:

1. Photo—of me with my husband Bill by a pond at a boarding school where I taught, up in the Berkshires when we'd been married about 6 years—so we'd be 27 years old. It's winter, we're both bundled up, Bill in a ski jacket and me in a woven multi-colored wool cape. We're holding hands. It's from a time when we shared mountain hikes, camping out, going for runs, but hadn't really been tested yet—we hadn't lost our parents or my brother, I hadn't gotten cancer. I like the thought of us then, but I like us—and our marriage—better now.

2. A memory—Boston Marathon, 3 years ago, my younger sister (14 years younger) is running the marathon to raise money for cancer research. She's wearing our mother's name on her front (Mother died of cancer) and my name on her back. She spots me in the crowd and starts yelling my name and pointing, and people in the crowd start yelling my name along with her. Then I yell her name—Ellen, Ellen!—and they pick up that chant, too. I feel very close to her always, but especially then. I was in tears but laughing, as well.

3. An activity—hiking in the mountains

4. Freewriting on choice 3: Mountain hiking has been an essential part of who I am, since the first family hikes in the Whites. My short, 8-year-old legs—they'll always be short—trying to keep up with younger brothers, especially Randy, who runs ahead and then back and then round us in circles, endless energy. Then summer camp in my early teens: no confidence, no canteen, no boots—just cheap, thin-soled sneakers—wondering if I'll make it to the top, never looking athletic like the other girls, but starting to love the exultant feel of bare rocks under my feet and sweeping views from the top. Then college: hiking the Green Mts. with Bill, new trails, still not trusting my endurance but loving the release you feel when you break out of the trees at timberline and get a sudden rush of wind, strength, speed, new life up there nearer the hawks and clouds. Years later I would be the one to lead, my body primed by daily running. Then cancer, but still the reassurance when energy returns that I can test myself and lose myself—and find myself—on trails again.

I've signed up the computer room for next morning, partly because this makes our interviewing seem more important, more professional. Also, it changes the venue, which for fourteen-year-olds is always a good thing. The printer is handy, too. Students will be printing out interview questions and answers for me as well as emailing them to their partners to check for factual accuracy. Dramatically, I announce the pairs. Then I ask partners to sit next to each other at the computers.

"Now listen, because this is a little complicated. You'll be doing several things by yourself before you and your partner start interviewing each other. Watch what Nick and I do. We exchange our writing from last night and read each other's three topics to see if we think our partner made a good final choice for us to focus on. I see Nick's chosen acting. His notes are already giving me some good insights into why he loves it, what it does for him, and how long it's been part of his life, so now I'm interested in finding out more."

"And yours looks good too, Ms. Michaels. Gee, you wrote a lot. This is gonna be easy!"

"Next, Nick and I are going to type up some questions we think we need to ask in our interviews, maybe to get more information about particular things our partner wrote or to clarify something we're not sure about. You'll probably find you need more *specific details* to make your subject come alive on the page. For instance, I'm going to ask Nick what plays he's been in, what roles, what his first musical was; his statement doesn't include those specifics, and I think readers will be interested. I'm going to *take a look into the future*—ask whether he wants to make a career in the theater. I might ask what he finds hardest about acting—so my piece will have *a little tension or conflict*, some obstacles for the hero to confront on his theatrical journey. Use your imagination; assume there's more to find out. Try to put yourself in your partner's place; what more might he or she have to tell? Also, put yourself in your readers' place: ask yourself what's missing that they might wonder about, that would help them get to know this person better."

Soon computer keys start to click. When I finish with Nick, I walk around, peering at screens and notes, giving specific praise and suggestions loudly enough so everyone can hear and get ideas. It's a kind of group conference. Once both partners have some questions up on the screen, I urge them to start the interviews.

Interviewing

"Looking good, Julia—very thoughtful questions about what's in Ayana's mind when she's going through the museum. Do you know yet if she has any favorite artists? Jess, I see Jenna's written you a very long statement about being a ninth grader on varsity field hockey, so you may have to choose one or two areas to focus your questions on. They seem like they're all over the map right now. What looks the most interesting? What's she seem to feel most strongly about? Garret, okay, you've started interviewing, but I see you're typing really short answers to your questions. Do you need Hunt to slow down and repeat things? Or do you need to ask him for more about each question? Figure it out."

Quoting

"Ms Michaels, how do we know when to type in their exact words, like a quote, and when we can just put it in our own words?"

"Wonderful question, Sydney. I'm sure a lot of you folks are wondering. So let's stop and figure this out. Here's a copy for each of you of the current *Spokesman*. Notice there are some short profiles on new teachers and on the foreign exchange student. Oh, and there's the Artist of the Month interview and Athlete of the Month. Pick one interview that looks interesting, skim it, and *underline all the quotations in it*—the places *where we actually hear the subject's voice*. Some of you, by the way, may want to think about trying out for the *Spokesman* staff. They don't take many ninth graders, but the ones they do take get to learn a lot about journalism and usually move up the ladder the following year."

As students read, I ask them to think about which quotes work the best. Are any of these not really pulling their weight? What makes a quote effective? We end up agreeing—and this will be useful when we start setting up assessment criteria for the project—that if the quote is worded in an interesting or memorable way, then it might be good to include.

"Or if it shows you the person's attitude," says Connor. "And Ms. Michaels, can we add gestures and expressions like the newspaper does—'she says with a little smile'—you know, like that?"

"Sure, Connor, if it's relevant, if it's not just a formula. And don't be afraid of the word *said* or *says*. You don't need fancy synonyms. William Zinsser, who's written a lot for *The New Yorker,* says this in his book *On Writing Well.* . . . Wait a minute, I know I brought that book in with me. Here:

> Don't strain to find synonyms for "he said" . . . and please!—don't write "he smiled" or "he grinned." I have never heard anybody smile. The reader's eye skips over "he said" anyway, so it's not worth a lot of fuss. If you crave variety, choose synonyms that catch the shifting nature of the conversation. "He pointed out," "he explained," "he replied," "he added"—these all carry a particular meaning. (91–92)

I think I'll photocopy a couple of pages from Zinsser for you to read and use over these next few days, about choosing and incorporating quotes. Just listen to how this bit expands on what we said about quoting: 'Single out the quotations that are most important or colorful. . . . Your job is to distil the essence. . . . Play with the quotes by all means—selecting, rejecting, thinning, transposing their order, saving a good one for the end. Just make sure the play is fair. Don't change any words or let the cutting of a sentence distort the proper context of what remains' (88–89). So if Hunt tells Garret one thing early in the interview and then says something that expands on that thing in answering a question later on, Garret can *combine* these two quotes. And something Hunt said in answering the *first* question might turn out to make a good *closing* quote for the profile. You've got some flexibility, in other words.

"One more thing: Are you all noticing the different ways these quotations are *introduced* in these interviews? You aren't given a lot of the raw interview—not 'I asked Nick . . . and he answered . . .' The profile would slow way down and get very repetitive if you left in all that scaffolding, and what would happen to the focus, which is meant to be on Nick?"

"Oh," says Ayana, "it would shift back and forth between you and him, wouldn't it?"

"Right. We know the profile will grow out of all the 'I asked and he said' but we don't need to *see* that. I'll leave most of that out so my profile stays focused on *Nick.* Oh, one more thing about using quotes: make the quote give us the information; don't introduce it with that *same* information, because then the quote becomes mere repetition. Like—I wouldn't write, 'Acting makes Nick notice things he wouldn't see otherwise. "Acting makes me notice things I wouldn't see otherwise," said Nick.'" General laughter. How could I think they would do anything that dumb?

I remind students that they should also look over their partner's written statement to see whether it contains any good lines to quote, not rely just on the interview. "I know a couple of points I'll probably quote from Nick's statement—what he says about needing to be calm right before he goes on stage and maybe also how acting allows him to open himself up to people. I think it's important to have these *in his own voice,* as they show his expertise and one reason he values acting." I'm noting these points on my clipboard for posting tonight as reminders.

By the end of the period, many students say they still need more material; they didn't get full enough answers or they didn't get to ask all their questions. "Okay, finish the rest of the interview by email. By class time tomorrow, I want you to have gathered all the information and quotations you need, and I want to see a draft started—at least half a page. That way, we'll have time in class to work with problems that arise tonight, to continue drafting on the laptops, and to have a quick lesson on leads or hooks." Each day at the end of class, I try to remember to clarify the *reasons* for that night's homework—its place in the process.

So Far/What Next?

While there are a lot of new things to learn for this project and various sets of notes and questions to juggle, most of the students seem interested. At the risk of stereotyping, I'd say that the boys like the challenge of gathering facts and being newspapermen, while the girls enjoy finding out about their partners' lives and feelings. I found myself asking boys, "So what thoughts were going through your head when your uncle took you hunting with him for the first time?" while with girls it was more apt to be, "So what, *specifically*, made summer camp so amazing and incredible, and what was so great about these tent mates you'll never ever forget?"

Studying Models

When the students arrive the next day, there's some groaning. "Ms. Michaels, I can't make it all fit together. I keep going question, answer, question, answer." This is what I want to hear. This is why I held off on any close analysis of models until the students felt a need for more direction. Without that motivation, kids get antsy very fast during close textual analysis.

"Right. I think this is where we look at some sample profiles by students. Here's one that Jeff Kowalski wrote last year on Sam Chertok—Jordan, you probably know Jeff. He's on the football team. Both these guys—he and Sam—love architecture, and they both ended up writing about it, like Brooks and Matt right now on baseball. Then here's a profile Sophia Weissman wrote about Tracy Rosen's love of photography. You'll meet Sophia because she's one of the writing mentors, and she's on the *Cymbals* staff—the literary magazine. She does Mock Trial and Model UN, too. And Tracy's photos are in *Cymbals*. Let's start with their *leads* or *hooks*. What do you notice in both profiles? Right. They both *start with quotes*: 'It's really cool to be able to capture a moment,' said Tracy, a small, reminiscent smile on her face, 'and keep it in a camera.' And Jeff starts his with 'It is a long way from the paper to the building,' said Sam Chertock, who dreams of becoming an architect some day.' Any thoughts about these two openings?"

Openings

"They're both great quotes," says Julia, "because they give you specific images. Not just 'she loves photography' or 'he loves architecture.' They both make those things sound interesting, even if you don't know much about them."

"Yeah, and they show attitude," Connor adds. "Tracy's smile is 'reminiscent,' not just any old smile. Like, just thinking about photography makes her happy. And, uh, you can tell Sam likes architecture because it's challenging."

"But I thought you always have to start a paragraph with a topic sentence," Garret protests.

"Well, the quotes kind of *are* topic sentences," Julia tells him. "They let you know what and who the profile's about." Garret still looks anxious.

"It makes sense," I tell them, "that as you are all becoming more experienced writers, trying a greater variety of pieces, you get to reinterpret the so-called rules. There are a lot of different ways to introduce the topic of a paragraph. These quotations are just another way. Donald Murray, who wrote a lot of great books on writing, says a good opening or "lead" for an essay 'should contain, or at least imply, a central tension—it might be irony or surprise or a problem or contradiction—that will be explored in the essay' (58). Now, your profiles are very short—just a page, not much time for exploring a central tension—but it's interesting that both Jeff's and Sophia's opening quotes imply a challenge or problem that Sam and Tracy see as central to their interests—moving from drawing to building and capturing and 'keeping' a moment in the camera."

Organization: The Writer's Journey

"Let's look at *structure* next. *Organization.* Where do these two profiles go after the opening quote? That's right, Jess, *backward*, into the past; so what question did the writers probably ask, at some point? Right—'How did you first get interested in this?' Which means the profiles can now move *forward*, if the writers want to. You don't *have* to move back to the past right off—there's no formula—but it's a natural choice, isn't it? Moving on from there, chronologically, can help your reader follow your points, whereas jumping around a lot in your subject's life could be confusing. Now, the big question: see if you can explain how Sophia and Jeff both avoid the question-and-answer pattern some of you got stuck in last night."

This is hard to articulate, but Peter comes through for us: "It's like, say you're writing a report on dinosaurs. You need to just stick to developing the information you have—the dinosaurs blah blah blah. And you expand as much as you need to on each point. And, uh, you arrange the points logically, so one leads into the next. You don't keep interrupting with 'And then I read some more in the encyclopedia and it said that dinosaurs blah blah blah.'"

"Does this make sense to you all?" I ask, wondering if Peter might like my job for the rest of the year. "Let's apply it to Jeff's profile: After he reports how Sam's uncle got him interested in architecture, he goes on to how Sam chose to take the first-year course here at school and then has Sam describe his favorite architectural project in the course so far—an interesting detail, a concrete example, right? Then he gives us a quote about how Sam loves the challenge of 'making what is on the paper come alive.' Notice how that reminds us of the hook: 'It's a long way from the paper to the building.' Jeff's giving this big single paragraph *coherence*, making it hold together. And then, at the very end, what does Jeff do? How does he *conclude?*"

Endings

"Ooh!" says Jess. "He goes *way* into the future. He says he expects that one day he'll be admiring this new museum or something and he'll go inside and see Sam's name as the designer on the plaque in the lobby. So he goes into the future."

"Great, Jess. So after the opening hook in the present with a hint of the future—Sam's 'dream'—the piece goes back to the past and just moves straight forward. But it ends with Jeff *imagining* Sam's future—and it's a very specific little scenario. He's empathized enough with Sam to imagine a scene and show it to us.

"Notice also that he doesn't write a dull little summarizing sentence: 'In conclusion, it can be seen that architecture is really important to Sam,' or a needless question with an obvious answer, like 'So what have we learned about Sam? That architecture is something he loves to do.' How many of you were taught that every piece of writing has to end with a summary? Was that a few years ago? Around the same time you learned about topic sentences? Right. But now, as you're writing in a whole bunch of different genres—interviews, monologues, personal stories—*you're ready to ask yourself whether each rule you've learned applies equally to every kind of writing*. Think about this for a minute: In what kind of piece might readers really *need* a closing summary? Imagine you've just read a complicated article of, say, twenty pages about three conflicting theories on how and why dinosaurs became extinct. At the end, you might be rather confused and very grateful for a quick, clear summary, yes? And presumably a judgment about which theory is most convincing. But our one-page profiles, assuming they're clearly organized, aren't going to confuse anyone. Our readers *don't need summaries*.

"Take a look at Sophia's ending. After she spends some time with Tracy's preferences—still life, black and white, 'making the ordinary special'—the piece moves ahead into a question about Tracy's future plans. So like Jeff, Sophia moves into the future. She ends with a quote—which is another choice you could make in your profile: 'Tracy says, "I am not motivated by entering competitions or winning prizes. My love of photography motivates me."' It's not a tacked-on ending but instead flows naturally from what came earlier: 'She loves photography because it lets her relive memories just by looking at her pictures. When asked if she has ever submitted her photographs to competitions, Tracy pauses, as if this is a question that she had pondered.' See how those sentences set us up for the final quote? That quote moves us on beyond specific details of her photography to an overarching statement of her love for it—a strong ending that leaves me with Tracy's voice in my ears and a belief in how much photography means to her, now and probably for years to come.

"Julia, may I use you as a test case? If Jess, let's say, reads your profile on Ayana, what would you like her to end up thinking, or feeling?"

"Well, maybe I'd want her to think, 'Gee, I feel like I know Ayana a little better.' . . . and, uh, 'I get how she felt in the museum seeing those paintings about war and hardships in different cultures.'"

"Great! So think about this when you write your ending. You all know how when you throw a pebble into a pond, it disappears but you see the ripples circling out from it? Suppose your reader's mind is the pond; what ripples do you want your pebble/interview to make?" Two days later, when I finish reading Julia's profile, I see she's chosen to end with a quote from Ayana that focuses us on exactly this point: "Most importantly, the paintings give Ayana a different outlook on the world: 'Paintings that portray war and hardships teach me about the different cultures and the stress in the world and this really opens my eyes. It gives me an opportunity to step back and appreciate what I have.'" I love Ayana's image of both physically and mentally stepping back, of gaining perspective on a painting and the world.

In these discussions of hooks and endings, we've really been talking about structure—where the "leads" might lead us and what the ending flows from. As we return to drafting, I suggest everyone might try putting their points in some kind of order first—no need for a formal outline, just a list. Then it seems like a natural time to look at sample transitions.

Transitions

"You saw how Jeff and Sophia moved back in time after their opening quotes, then straight ahead, and near the end moved into the future. They *signaled* these moves to you so you wouldn't be confused, and I think you can spot those signals. Let's look at my profile of Nick for something a little more complicated. See how I start by quoting his story about when he was five years old? How do I signal I'm moving forward to a number of different ages? Right, James—'ever since that trip.' That lets me pick any point between five and the present, but I need to indicate how old he is in the present, which I do—'Now at fourteen.' Then where? Right—'in fifth grade.' Want to underline these time change signs with me? Where's the next one? Okay, 'for three straight years.' Now, toward the end I want to move to the future. How do I do that? Right, Brooks, 'next year.' But then I go back to the present—'but for now.' And then I go to the recent past—'recently' he's taken a workshop. And then he's 'just' read—like maybe the last few days? And then the near future—'this winter he will . . .' And finally I start traveling backward, wishing I'd seen him in earlier shows—'in last year's eighth-grade show' and 'maybe even better . . . in the fourth-grade operetta'—two kinds of transitions there, 'better' for comparison and 'fourth-grade' for time, right? And for my ending, I step back and take in all I've learned about his career with 'so far.'"

I've been writing these key words on the board as I read them, so when the kids look up from underlining, they can see the range of times and transitions. "Before I started drafting, I really had to make a list—not a formal outline, just a list—of the events in the order I planned to use them, and then figure out where I'd need to signal the time jumps. Is it clear enough, do you think?"

"Yeah, Ms. M.," Nick says enthusiastically.

"Well, it should be for you, Nick. This is your life! Now do you all feel ready to make your lists and try out some transitions? If you did half a draft last night, you can start listing from that and change your order if you need to." The room gets quiet, with just occasional interruptions when writers realize they need to clear up a point with their partner. At the end of class, I ask students to complete a draft for peer response tomorrow but also to make a list of what they think the criteria should be for assessing these pieces.

Creating Criteria

I ask the students to review the models—Sophia's, Jeff's, mine—but also to draw on things they like about their own draft and then to email me at least six criteria. "Imagine yourself as the *reader*. Think what qualities would make a profile you would enjoy reading. But also think, as the *writer*, of these qualities being goals you're trying to reach in your piece." I also explain that the lists shouldn't include usage items—syntax and grammar, punctuation, spelling, capitalization. We'll work on these all year, both in mini-lessons and conferences; they're important. But right now, I want everyone to peer edit and revise using the criteria they've been discovering these last few days, not get sidetracked by correcting—or, in many cases, mis-correcting—usage errors.

From the lists that students email me that night, plus a couple points of my own, I cobble together a peer response sheet. Of the usual rubric terms or traits—content, organization or development, voice, word choice, sentence fluency—I put down only those that students send me. Some of their items are *related* to voice; it's just not a term they're used to. Their lists include: *quotations that show attitude, quotations worded well, catchy hook or topic sentence, putting points in a clear order, interesting details/examples, help-ful transitions, a nonsummary ending that* (several kids remembered my im-age) *makes ripples*. Not everyone was equally articulate, but they were all in the same ballpark. I add three more items of my own: (1) clear, smooth, and varied incorporation of quotes (which I know will take months, years, for some of them to master, but we may as well get started on it); (2) consistent focus on topic throughout; and (3) an effective title (okay, the *sub*title can be "Profile of Sarah").

For some of the students, the concept of peer response is new, and for many putting it into practice is very difficult, both socially and intellectu-ally. Having helped create the criteria gives the students more interest in applying them, both to their partner's work and their own. It also moves us closer to one of my goals for the year—establishing a studio atmosphere.

Peer Response

Next day I compliment students on their thoughtful criteria, and we take turns reading aloud from the peer response sheets (see Figure 2.2).

First, as the author, fill out this sheet at the top with at least one criterion for which you'd like feedback and suggestions—one that's giving you
trouble. Your partner will make sure to respond to this first. Now give
this sheet to your partner along with your profile draft. Because you're
reading what your partner wrote about *you* from the interview, your
first silent reading will be for fun and to satisfy your curiosity. Does this
profile look like, sound like, you? Are all the facts and quotes accurate?
Read with a pencil and just put a little *X* next to any that aren't. But
mainly, read for enjoyment—as if this were an interview in one of your
favorite magazines.

   Now read it a *second* time, and just put an * next to any word,
phrase, sentence, or passage that you admire for the writing craft and
a *zzz* next to any that strikes you as filler, wordy, boring, in need of
tightening, or that includes interview scaffolding like "I asked him and
he replied." This is a preliminary gut response, but it's the start of being
a good critic, spotting the strengths and weaknesses and reading as a
writer.

   On your *third* reading, write in responses to the specific criteria on
the peer response sheet. Wherever you're asked to make suggestions,
write those in the margins of the drafts; use arrows, if that's helpful.

FIGURE 2.2. PEER RESPONSE DIRECTIONS.

"I know some of you aren't used to writing on another person's paper,"
I tell them, "but these are just rough drafts and need to be marked up. Your
partner's doing the same for you. Remember, you're not editing for usage errors here; you're responding to the piece as a whole and then to the specific
criteria you all set up; don't get sidetracked.

"Learning to be a good peer responder is crucial for your own growth as
a writer. Research has shown [and here I put on a deep, big-time Researcher
voice] that the ability to respond critically to someone else's writing carries
over to recognizing what works and doesn't work in your own. It's usually
easier to get some critical distance on another person's piece than on yours.
So see how helpful a reader you can be. When both of you have finished,
return the profile and response sheet, read what your partner has said, and
if anything seems unclear, have a brief, very quiet conversation. Then I'll

ask you to write on the back of the response sheet which specific comments you think you can use in revising."

When I don't add that last step—assessing the peer response—kids give and receive much less focused, specific, and responsible feedback. I also make sure, when the revised draft is turned in, to ask the writer to do a little self-assessing: to list on the back some strengths in the piece and at least one area of concern that he or she would work on more if there were time. This helps me focus my reading, assessing, and conferring and helps the writer weigh the possibilities of further revision. Below the directions I include questions based on our criteria (see Figure 2.3).

---

1. Are there facts or quotations that need correcting?____ If so, mark them on the draft with an *X*, and write or tell your partner what needs to be changed.
2. Are there at least three quotations from the interviewee?____ Does each quotation help convey his or her attitude/feelings/character, not just factual information? ____If not, mark on the draft with a question mark.
3. Are the quotations incorporated smoothly, without the scaffolding of "I asked" and "she answered"? ____ Mark with a *Q* any that could be incorporated better, and discuss with your partner.
4. What areas need to be expanded, "cracked open," with more specific details or more indication of the interviewee's attitudes, feelings, thoughts? Mark these with an *E* for Expand. Might this require further interviewing?
5. Does the profile cohere, that is, stay focused and progress with helpful transitions?_____ Is the order of ideas and facts effective? Write your suggestions on the draft, and discuss as necessary.
6. Effective title?___ Catchy and focusing hook?_____ Effective non-summary, "ripple effect" ending? Make suggestions for improving any of these on the draft.

FIGURE 2.3. *PEER RESPONSE QUESTIONS.*

Conference during Peer Response

I need to reinforce the importance of second and third peer readings. As I start circling the room, I notice that Jordan hasn't put any stars or *zzz*'s on Connor's draft. "How come, Jordan?"

"Oh, he said not to."

"How come, Connor?"

"Well, I might want to turn it in just as it is. I think it's pretty good."

I know, from reading his response to the poem our first night, that Connor is sensitive to language; he seems to be a thoughtful writer. "Would you mind if I took a quick skim?"

"Sure."

When I finish reading, I ask Jordan, "What do you think about this profile's ending? The very last sentence. What's it doing?"

"Well, it's going over the things I told Connor I remember best about my uncle. I guess it's sort of a summary."

"Yes. And Connor, how does it connect to the sentence right before it, about Jordan's mom?"

"I guess it doesn't," Connor says. "I just needed an ending."

"So Jordan, that might be one criterion to make a suggestion about? And Connor, an area to work on, maybe?" Then I notice that Jordan's draft is handwritten and very short.

"Are you planning to write more, Jordan? Do you need to ask Connor more questions?" As I skim, I'm starting to suspect that the two boys haven't found much common ground yet. Connor chose his two-week safari to Africa with his grandparents as the topic for Jordan to interview him about; Jordan chose his memories of his late uncle, who served as a father to him while his mother and grandmother worked in his grandfather's restaurant. Each needs to ask the other more questions. Jordan seems comfortable talking about feelings. Glancing at his interview questions and answers, I see that he asked Connor to talk about his relationship with his grandparents and why they wanted to take him to Africa, but Connor offered very little. On the other hand, Connor overlooked, or chose not to quote, a moving line Jordan wrote in his initial statement about the impact of his uncle's death that might have made an effective ending for the profile: "It still is really difficult for me as well as my family to try to remember him and not feel incredibly sad." It would flow naturally from some of the memories Connor has recorded.

Other contrasts: Connor's writing is highly fluent, as were most of his answers that I overheard during the first interview session; Jordan, on the other hand, wrote down some pretty vague versions of Connor's answers—"C. talked about the leader in Zimbabwe and their struggles"—but he may have been embarrassed to ask his partner to repeat or explain. Jordan seems to write the way he speaks—sentences run together, a lot of fragments, many lines starting with "Well"—yet he offers complicated emotional truths: "I often thought my mom was innocently jealous. Of how when I was very young I would sometimes run straight to my uncle." I'm struck by the insight and the caring of that "innocently jealous." Connor is, so far, well organized, whereas Jordan has already lost Connor's initial statement (and will later lose the peer response sheet). It's clear that they have very different kinds of strengths and come from different backgrounds; I'm hoping that more interview time will help them communicate better.

And, in fact, given an extension on their deadline, both manage to acquire more information. Jordan, asking Connor about the African people he met, gets a description of how "weird" it felt that fifteen people would live in a single village hut and how in one of them "a mother was watching her baby playing with a knife and didn't seem worried, just threw the knife thoughtlessly across the crowded room." The "felt weird" suggests Connor's discomfort with the contrast between village poverty and the comforts of his safari, a discomfort that may have been awkward for him to elaborate on to Jordan. I sense some frustration with the interview when Jordan writes, "Connor didn't really say how the other natives except the guide treated him, there was just this one incident with the mother that he felt the need to express." Connor, in turn, asked Jordan how he thinks his life would be different if his uncle were still alive, a question that may well have been an emotional reach for Connor. Later, in his revision, he quotes Jordan's answer: "It would probably be less stressed because everybody went to him with their troubles . . . like when I would have a problem dealing with schoolwork, he would help me through it and help me get better."

The two boys' work on this project shows me how much writing can reveal—and how complicated the process of connecting with a stranger can be. Despite Jordan's and Connor's difficulties, I think both boys grew, as people and as writers, from having to make this connection, and that as they sit in class the rest of the year participating in discussions, they'll listen to each other's voices with more understanding than if they hadn't written each other's profile.

Assessing, Revising, Assessing

This is the stage in the writing process where things get messiest and most frustrating, especially with ninth graders and especially with their first effort at peer response. As I looked over shoulders, I could see that some kids had gotten sidetracked by the urge to "correct" errors. Quiet, meticulous Matt had created new errors in trying to fix Brooks's punctuation, and he had completely missed the awkward presence of question-and-answer scaffolding, the weak hook, and the summary ending. Jenna, who had enthusiastically starred a lot of Jess's strong details and had noted some repetitive quotations (*zzz*), had then been unable to resist correcting comma "errors"; later she would reveal herself to be the queen of comma splices. James had corrected a few spelling errors in Peter's piece on biking but hadn't recognized the need for more specific details. Nearly everyone had made good suggestions about drab (or missing) titles and dull or unfocused hooks. And since most students had chosen effective quotes, that criterion didn't need much work from the responders. But very few students were helpful, as yet, with more global revisions. They weren't visualizing how a sentence could be moved farther down to make the time sequence clearer or to lead more effectively toward the closing sentence. They weren't hearing how six short sentences in succession, all starting with subject and verb, drained half the piece of its energy.

Why were they being such passive readers? Did they assume anything in print was finished, unchangeable? Or was it a lack of motivation to help their peers? Discomfort with offering—and receiving—negative feedback? Inexperience as responders and revisers? Probably all of the above. When I asked at the end of the period what feedback they'd found helpful and planned to use in revising, the list we ended up with was short: *better title and/or subtitle, stronger opening hook, find a good quote or question to end with,* and (vaguely) *better transitions.* Still, it was a start—an admission that there was some point in going back to the drawing board.

Sharing Revisions

But these young writers need to do more than incorporate peer suggestions. I want them to take on the responsibility for considering how well their own draft meets our criteria. So I transform the peer response sheet back into a simple checklist. The assignment for tonight is twofold (see Figure 2.4). This is also the week we hold our first one-on-one conferences, during part of a shared free period, lunch, a study hall, or before or after school. In conference, I'll focus on students' awareness of the changes they've made and their reasons for making them, along with some discussion of peer response—theirs and their partner's. I'll also make time for some conversation about what kinds of reading and/or writing they like best. I want to keep each student's preferences in mind (including their preferred mediums) as we move toward the free-choice project.

Next day nearly everyone has a new draft. "So let's hear which of your changes you like best. And maybe when you tell us, you could also say who you profiled and what your 'angle' or 'lens' was." I want them to feel they're getting immediate follow-up since some will have to wait for feedback from me until we find a conference time. I get the students down on the floor in a tight circle to help them concentrate on listening to one another and to dramatize that this is an important moment to share as a writing community—the first revision, the first submission of a piece of writing. It's also a chance to learn more about one another as we listen to the subjects that we each chose to be interviewed about.

1. Read your draft *aloud, slowly,* with a piece of paper covering up all but the line you're reading, to focus you and slow you down. Read with your checklist and your partner's peer response sheet at your elbow and a pencil in your hand. REVISE.
2. When you've strengthened the piece as much as you can in one night, print out the new draft, attach it to the old one along with the peer edit sheet and checklist (checked off), and write on the back:
   a. changes you've made—and why
   b. at least one thing you'd like to work on more and/or get help with

FIGURE 2.4. CHECKLIST FOR REVISING.

Connor likes his new ending, replacing the summary sentence with a question about how the death of Jordan's uncle will affect him in the future. A few kids look over at Jordan, taking in this new information about someone they mainly know so far as a football player.

"I had to cut *a lot,*" Jess says. "I got so much material from Jenna on varsity field hockey that I wrote, like, seven big paragraphs, but when I read it over, the key thing was how Jen could share in the closeness of the team, even though she's just a freshman, so I cut things she said about all her past years in hockey and some stuff I said twice about the tough practices and coaches. So I like how it fits together now."

"My profile on Sarah and the photo of her dancing with her uncle was way too short," Jessica says. "So I looked at the criteria about details and put in more description of the photo—about how Sarah is so small she just comes up to his knee, and she's in this long, grown-up pink dress. And I emailed her for some more details of stuff they used to do together when he was still alive." I'm pleased that Jessica's speaking up. This is the first time she's joined in whole-group discussion since the pebble/marble game. Sarah looks over at Jordan, catches his eye, and smiles; she realizes they've both lost uncles they were close to.

Matt's pleased with his ending. "I kept the idea but I just changed the wording because one word didn't sound right."

"Maybe you could read the two versions for us, Matt?" I want him to get comfortable talking to the class and get them to listen to this new student with the very quiet voice.

Matt flushes, gulps, and reads: "'This is a remarkable story that involves great pain, an almost career-ending injury, and a dramatic baseball game. Even though he should be proud of himself for his courage, Brooks still describes the day as the worst of his life.' And in the rough draft I had: 'Even though this compliments him in many ways, Brooks still describes'—and so on." The guy sitting closest to Brooks whacks him on the back. We all know about the injury, and that baseball may be out of the picture for Brooks for the rest of the year.

"Yes, 'This compliments' sounds awkward, and your 'this' is vague, since I guess it refers to the whole situation or profile. 'Proud of himself for his courage' is much more specific and clear. Does anybody have any thoughts about the sentence Matt wrote to lead into that one—the 'pain, career-ending injury, dramatic game' sentence?"

"Yes, it's really great," Julia says, and Matt looks down at the floor. "It's got a big contrast, so it makes the story sound dramatic. And I like how Matt shows his feelings about Brooks having courage. It's a good personal way to end."

"Let me ask you all one more thing." With their free-choice project coming up in a few months, I want them each time we write a piece to think about what they've learned from it that might come in handy later. "If you were choosing your own piece to write—say, a short story, or some poems or song lyrics, or a personal experience of your own, or a scene for a play, or maybe an editorial—what have you learned, or worked on in this profile that could help you? Let's freewrite about this in our writer's notebook for a few minutes."

I write with them. Five minutes later we start a list on the board, and by the end of class we've created the list shown in Figure 2.5. Students turn in their profiles. "I'm excited to read these," I tell them. "If you get an idea

1. Using quotes—good for dialogue or for evidence in anything ("Can you use dialogue in a poem?" asks Julia, and I promise to email them all some examples, starting with "Jabberwocky")
2. Specific details—good for describing places or characters or real people; for evidence; for an image in a poem
3. Good opening hook—good for anything
4. Ending that's not a summary, that leaves you thinking—good for anything
5. Putting points in a good order—good for anything ("But for a poem, Ms. Michaels? How about in haiku?" Julia persists. "Well, Julia, it might not be a logical or chronological order—it might be the way your thoughts jump, or a connection through images and the senses, like in a movie or painting—but it should be a **good** order, effective in some way, right? It should serve the piece well.")
6. Transitions/flow—good for anything
7. Cutting repetition or irrelevant points—good for anything ("But," I forestall Julia, "some repetition can be very effective, especially in poems.")

FIGURE 2.5. WHAT STUDENTS LEARNED FOR LATER USE.

for more changes during our conference, or even a month later, the piece will be in your writing folder on my desk, still open for revising. You might even decide to take it to the Writing Center for a conference with one of the older student mentors. I'll be introducing you to a few of them pretty soon. The pieces of my own that get published or that I choose to save usually go through a lot of changes, especially the poems, sometimes over several years, at the same time as I'm writing new ones. So your future revising of this piece, if you do any, may well have to overlap with starting the next piece. We'll assess the profile together in conference, using our list of criteria. It will get a letter grade in light pencil, what I call a ghost grade, and your peer response for your partner will get a check or check-plus or plus. The ghost grade stays in my grade book but can change if you turn in a strong revision later on. I can make time to read one more new version and reassess—but only up till the week before term ends. If you're willing, I'll make a copy of your present version, though, so we can have a class anthology of profiles and get to read everyone's. Yes, Garret?"

"We could make it a party. With cupcakes."

"No. Pizza," Brooks says firmly.

Assessing in Conference

Whoever said that the best learning takes place with two people on either end of a log would understand the power of the student–teacher writing conference. As teachers we all need this precious opportunity to listen: to a student read aloud from a paper or notebook and maybe pick his favorite sentence, or try out an idea for a personal story, introduce us to a favorite writer, even moan about writer's block. I learn a lot from hearing what a kid thinks her convoluted sentence is saying, and I love the sudden breakthrough moment when *she* suggests a colon might work better than a comma right there where she'd created the run-on. It's almost criminal that, given the average teaching load in schools throughout the country, these moments are so hard for most of us to come by. In my first teaching job in a large school in California, where I had five classes of 35 to 40 students each, regular conferences were impossible. Pundits who insist that class size has little effect on the quality of student writing have simply never tried to teach 175 teenagers to write. In my present school, those colleagues with a full course load either rotate their conferences, seeing each class every four weeks, or else they let students sign up, and require a set number of conferences per term. I try to meet each ninth grader (not my older students) every two weeks, at least for the first couple of months. I expect them to learn, gradually, to use the Writing Center, do a better job with peer response, and take on more responsibility for their revising.

This morning I'm having my first conference with Peter, the bright, home-schooled new student who came up with the dinosaur example the other day. I'm not sure he's made friends yet with any other ninth graders. I'd like to help him connect with a few of the juniors and seniors on the newspaper staff.

As we talk, I learn that he read *I, Claudius* and *Great Expectations* last spring and is currently halfway through *Pride and Prejudice*. He may be the first ninth-grade boy I've met who's chosen to read Austen. Since he says he's enjoying her wit, I suggest Twain's *A Connecticut Yankee in King Arthur's Court* for a different satiric voice and write the title in the front of his binder, which I notice is pretty chaotic. "Think you can get that organized tonight, Peter? It will make life much easier for you. I give a lot of handouts that need to be fastened in or they'll get lost. I don't see James's peer response sheet attached to your revision either. Can you find that and put it on my desk? It's already a day late. I need to see what use you made of it, and I'll want to discuss it with James, too."

"Uh, okay, sure. I'm not really used to notebooks or all these extras for a paper. At home I just used a couple of drawers for my stuff."

"So tell me your thoughts about your profile on James and the family fishing trips. What parts of the process worked for you? What do you like about this draft, and is there anything you might still want to revise?"

"I think James's notes helped me with the interview. And with the writing, too, because he included a lot of details and used all the senses. I did mean to go back to him with a few more questions, but I never got around to it. I used a good quote from the interview, though—when I asked if catching his own food contributed to the experience of the trip."

"Yes. And you used it well, right near the end. 'I'm not a big fish or seafood guy, but it's kinda cool catching your own food.' It definitely captures James's voice. Let's go through the checklist of criteria together: *at least three quotations worded well? showing attitude?*—You've got how many?"

"Um, one. Yeah, I should get some more."

"Okay. And *a catchy hook/topic sentence*? 'Fishing is more than just a sport to James Sanderson—it is a way his family comes together and bonds.' Are you happy with that?"

"I think so. Because it's what the profile's all about, and it gets two ideas in, that contrast, sort of."

"Yes, that's an excellent analysis. And your *ending expands on it, illustrates it*, with a really neat turn of phrase: 'After working and having fun together, and enjoying the fruits (or in this case, fish) of their labor, his entire family is closer.' I love 'the fish of their labor' and I also think you're handling your sentence structure well, starting with the participial phrases and saving your main point for that little five-word main clause for the close of the sentence, the strongest position. So we can check off your *hook* and *closing*. How about *order of your points*?"

Peter skims the page. "Yeah, I think it's clear. I get his childhood fishing in early, then the lake fishing, then the focus on saltwater fishing, then the description of the ocean trip and the outdoor barbecuing near the end."

"Excellent. And when I read it aloud last night, it flowed smoothly. You've got time *transitions* where you need them—'when he was six, ever since, often, at the end of the day, on his latest trip.' And as we look at the order, I also notice lots of good details about the trip. So we can check off *details*. I really like that sentence about the barbecue a lot—'At the end of the day, although the fishing trip is over, this domestic festival is not.' I like the little chime of the *est* sound in *domestic festival*. And the phrase sounds sort of Latinate."

Peter grins. "James liked that, too. But Ms. Michaels, one thing that's not on the checklist but I'm noticing it now, there's an awful lot of 'fish,' 'fishing,' 'fishermen.'"

"Good for you! The repetition. I noticed that, too, and wondered if you had read it aloud."

"Nope. I guess I should. Can I fix that? I can't think what other words to use, though."

"I know. In the eighteenth century, you'd have said 'the finny prey.' Or there's 'piscine,' right? I think you might have fun looking for synonyms, but I'll bet you can also just do some cutting and condensing. For instance, see that sentence a third of the way down? 'They board a hired boat and head out onto the sunny sea for a full day of fishing.' You said 'fishing' just before that, so one of those references could go. Now back to the checklist—I think full credit on *smooth incorporation of quotes*, on *consistent focus throughout*, and on *effective title*. So the only weak spot was shortage of quotes. What ghost grade do you think?"

Is it hypocritical to encourage a student to engage, heart and mind, with shaping a paper into an imaginative work of art and then categorize it with a single letter? I've tried grading content and style separately but ended up feeling that separating them sends the wrong message about the writing process, as if content comes first and is then poured into a container. My own experience as a writer tells me that the imagination is continually fusing the two, or, to put it another way, each is continually transforming the other. My insistence that the students participate in creating criteria out of their own experience with drafting each new piece and then apply these criteria in peer response, revising, and final assessments is an effort to make the grading as transparent and organic as possible. I want my writers to feel that the grade is only a small part of the conference, flows naturally from our joint application of the criteria, and is not set in stone. One could argue that asking a student to suggest a grade will just lead to grade grubbing and is a cop-out on the teacher's part, but I have rarely found this to be the case, provided the criteria were clear and established early in the writing process and that there is an opportunity for further revision.

"Maybe a B+?" says Peter, after a pause.

"Yes, that sounds about right to me, if we factor in the missing peer response sheet along with the shortage of quotations. And the repetition is a whole extra issue—not one of the criteria but well worth working on. I'll be happy to read a new draft and reassess once you've solved that and used a couple more quotes effectively. And if you start *Connecticut Yankee*, tell me what you think. Read parts of it aloud. It's even funnier that way." (Come November, Peter will choose to write a satiric fantasy in which the Greek gods return to earth. Twain will have left his mark.)

I've got Garret coming next, a whole different kettle of fish. In his profile on Hunt's love of climbing mountains, he mentions that he himself has climbed in the Adirondacks. Maybe he likes mountain books. I can suggest Jon Krakauer's *Into Thin Air*. But Garret's going to need a lot of help with sentence structure, as we work from the checklist on *incorporation of quotations* and *use of transitions*. I think we'll start with his reading the piece aloud, though I sense a tin ear at work. We'll close the door to prevent distraction. If only I had some cupcakes.

Part Three–Putting Us in the Zone: Describing, Reflecting

In the Art Zone

"Your assignment is to create a perfect circle using only a twig and ink. Every mark must be different and you cannot make lines," Mr. Hirniak's voice repeated in my head. After a few minutes of simply marking the paper it became a pattern. I would mark quickly, each time using a different angle or side of the twig. Soon, the room got very quiet. The sound of cars passing by and people walking past the classroom stopped. Mr. Hirniak's voice disappeared. All I could hear was the twig hitting the paper. The smell of ink filled the room. A circle was swiftly formed and for the rest of the period I expanded and filled in little spaces. "Denser, denser," Mr. Hirniak said repetitively. The twig was an extension of my hand and all I knew to do was mark and mark and mark. All I could see was the paper and although there was ink all over my hands I did not notice. I filled in every visible white space in my circle, trying to make it ideal. I did not know how to stop and I had no other thoughts but making a perfect circle. The rough twig scratched against my fingers but I barely noticed. I was completely dedicated and focused on my perfect circle.

Jessica Castello, grade 9

Commentary

Our second writing assignment, "In the Zone," is designed to move each student out of the reporter role and inward, to memory and reflection. Then outward again, as the writer imagines an audience and seeks language to communicate the memory of being "in the zone." As with the profile, a number of writing modes overlap in this assignment. The piece will show us a real person—the author—through the lens of an activity that fully engages her, but rather than *reporting* on it, working primarily with facts and quotation, she will rely on *evocative description*—sensory details, image and metaphor, shifting prose rhythms—to re-create the strange mix of concentration and relaxation, of time moving slowly . . . quickly . . . of complete timelessness, that has been characterized by Mihaly Csikszentmihalyi as "flow." This is a piece in which prose and poetry can join hands.

Jessica had been one of the quietest students in the class so far. I really had little impression of her yet. But sooner or later, if writing opportunities are sufficiently varied, most students will find their way to self-expression. Jessica was to make great strides as a writer in the course of the year, but this is the piece that gave her confidence that she *had* a voice and that helped me get to know her. Maybe the act of remembering how it *felt*—that fluid, concentrated marking with the twig to shape a circle—released some tension Jessica associated with writing and allowed her thoughts to flow onto the page.

In the Reading Zone—Reading as Writers

I introduce this assignment via our regular independent reading time, the first five or six minutes of every class period. I read along with the students, my writer's notebook open to record anything that catches my interest, particularly as a writer. I ask them to read as writers—to collect at least one item each day from their reading and put it in their notebooks—something that stops them for a moment, a word, a turn of phrase, an image, a bit of dialogue, an idea. Just now I'm in the middle of *Note by Note*, by a piano teacher in New Jersey, Tricia Tunstall, who creates such vivid sketches of her individual students' lessons that I feel as though I'm there in her music room, watching and listening. I ask all my readers to hold up their book and tell us why they chose it—one more way to build a writing community. "Just out of curiosity, how many of you have a strong preference for true stories rather than fiction?" A lot of boys' hands go up. "And the fiction lovers? Wait, let's break it down a bit. Who loves fantasy—like Tolkien's Ring Trilogy? Anybody read Ursula Le Guin? I finally read *Wizard of Earthsea* this summer and would really like to talk about it with someone. Okay, and what about science fiction? People who like one of those two genres don't always like the other. And adventure or suspense? Mysteries? Romance? Horror? Combinations—like the vampire books?" Lots of enthusiastic squeals. "Novels about families and relationships?" At least ten girls' hands go up. "How about plays? Poetry? Remind me to give you some great poetry websites. Magazines? Anybody read the dictionary? Try it. Graphic novels?

Who likes e-books better than print? How about audiobooks? They're especially fun if you're reading poems or a play. Anyone get the news online? Any newspaper fans?" The "reading zone," to borrow Nancie Atwell's term, is a place some of these kids may never have entered. But I know they're more likely to experience it with books they've discovered for themselves.

I give them some specific suggestions for reading as writers: "Watch for an interesting word to copy down—maybe it's new to you, or one you'd never have thought to use, or not use in this way, or maybe you like the sound, or it really fits the character using it, or it describes something perfectly, or you like the way it's combined with another word. Copy at least part of the sentence it's in so you'll have the context. You'll remember it better that way, and maybe you can try using it in a piece of your own. Next week let's put some of these collected words up on the wall. If you read a whole sentence that you think is strong for its sound or idea, jot that sentence down. Try reading with your ears wide open so you can hear the characters' voices, as if you were eavesdropping or could talk back to them. Hear when the pace picks up or slows down. Have you ever noticed how parts of a book move faster than other parts? Why is that, do you think? Is it you or the writer?"

We've read for four minutes or so. I've copied down a sentence I like for the contrasting sounds. Tunstall is describing one of her piano students: "Clearly, her years with pop crooners have not rendered her tone deaf to the somber beauty of Shostakovich" (86). I love the quick plosives and *oo* vowels of *pop crooners* contrasting to the dark, heaviness of *somber*, to the deep *o* at the back of the throat, the lingering *mb* and *r*. I like the strength and efficiency of the whole sentence. But I'd rather have a *student* model the stealing process than do it myself, so when I notice a couple of students writing, I call a halt. I ask Ayana whether she would mind sharing what she wrote down and talk about why she chose it.

Student Modeling

Ayana is well into Obama's *Dreams from My Father* and reads aloud in a voice I can barely hear: "How could we go about stitching a culture back together after it was torn?"

"Ayana, could you take a deep breath and push that sentence out one more time all the way across the room to Nick? It's worth our hearing." She tries, and amps it up a few decibels, maybe. "Why did you copy it down?"

"Well," Ayana says hesitantly, "it seems like such a hard question, but it's so important that he's asking it."

"I read the book over the summer, Ayana, and I thought that was one of the great things about it—the questions he's asking. Even if there aren't any easy answers, we'll never find any at all if we don't ask the questions, right? Did you like the way he worded that question?" I didn't want to push her, but it was a good chance to look at metaphor.

"Oh, I didn't think about that. Well, I guess, uh, sometimes it's easy to mend a rip, but maybe not this big a tear between, you know, different races. Maybe the stitches wouldn't hold. . . . I mean, we do keep trying to mend it. . . ."

"Did anybody besides me notice how Ayana took up Obama's metaphor and used it to do her own thinking?"

"Yes," says Julia, who's later going to prove herself a promising poet. "She used his sewing metaphor—the rip and tear and the stitches. You know, I can kind of feel the rip, like a wound, all bloody, that you have to close with stitches, and the stitches would hurt." I put the sentence up on the wall along with Ayana's name and the book title and author. Next to them I write "using a metaphor (figure of speech) to think with and to make readers think and feel." It's hard enough for kids to slow down and try to hear language on a page, but twice as hard for them to find words to *describe* what they're hearing and what effect it's having on them. So it's important to model this second half of the process.

"Whenever someone shares from a book after outside reading," I tell them all, "listen hard and add their word or sentence to your own list—with the book and author. You may even decide you'd like to read that book. I'll ask each of you to give me a guided tour of your reading notes at our next conference."

In the Reading Zone

We could have opened up Ayana's sentence to a discussion of racism, but it's early in the year for ninth graders to be comfortable sharing their thoughts on this topic, and anyway, I want to move them toward the next writing assignment—"a time you were in the zone." So I introduce the concept of "the reading zone." "Do you ever really get into a book so totally that you don't want to put it down? You don't even notice if you're being called to dinner or told that time's up? What's that feel like? And how does it happen?"

"Well, I'm easily distracted," Hunt admits. "And for me, it's really hard to read in class when I know there's only, like, five minutes. But at home, at night, if it's the right book, I can just cruise right along and suddenly it's bedtime and I haven't done half my homework." I write *cruise right along* and *time passes without your knowing it* up on the board. Someone else says that it's like when you're playing in a game and you make all the right passes and are in the right places on the field without having to think about it.

"And you're so into it," says Sydney, a varsity hockey player, "that you don't notice you're tired or that it's about 100 degrees on the field."

"With reading," says Julia, "you're sometimes inside the book, right in that world, and all that matters is what's going to happen next to this character." Several students are rolling their eyes as if Julia's just sprouted blue antennae.

"Can you be in the zone even if something's really hard?" I ask. Matt raises his hand politely.

"It's got to be something you know how to do, I think," he said, "something you love doing so you're throwing yourself into it and, uh, maybe it's challenging but when you're in the zone the hard parts feel easy." A lot of kids nod.

"So you could be in the zone if you're reading a book that's pretty hard, as long as it interests you?" I ask.

"Yeah, you probably just skim over the hard parts if they're boring," Jess says, laughing. "But," she adds, "it helps if it's a book you chose for yourself. I guess that's like a sport you choose to play. Nobody's forcing you."

"Could you move into the zone while you're learning something new and you catch on and start trying to do it on your own?" I ask, really curious about this one. There's a long silence. Then Peter's hand goes up.

"I think so," he says. "When I started to learn Latin, I really got into the translating homework, even though we started with single sentences, not stories or anything. It was like a puzzle I had to solve, and I'd get on a roll where I'd see how all the pieces in a sentence were fitting together. It was intriguing, I guess, to work out the meanings."

I want the students to explore this concept partly because I want them to recognize and value the joy of "losing" themselves in something, of living in the moment. I don't want their education to be focused on the next term grade, standardized test, college transcript, career. They'll meet these future events naturally and as successfully as their trained abilities allow if I can just help them experience fully the particular poem they're reading, the piece they're writing, the conversation we're having. I'm with John Dewey: education should be a continuous process of growth, not simply preparation. Yes, I'm preparing the students as well as I can to create a satisfying "free choice" piece a few months from now, and a final exam project in June that integrates and transforms some of the year's learning, but I want each separate assignment and process throughout the year to be a meaningful experience, rewarding in itself.

Criteria for Describing "In the Zone"

One of the challenges of this little piece will be capturing both the physical and the mental sensations of the zone—finding sensory details, figurative language, even sentence rhythms to "put a reader into the experience" without turning the piece into a narrative report of a game, a fishing trip, a piano recital. I hope the limitation to one typed page will help students stay focused. Like the profile, it's a new kind of writing for many of these kids, not simply description of a place or object, which many elementary school children are asked to do, but rather the challenge of describing a mental or emotional state. So as we talk, I ask what they think they can do, as writers, to bring their zone experience to life for the rest of us. I want them to share in establishing goals and criteria, as they did for the profile. By the end of the period, we have a list: *use the five senses, make comparisons, make contrasts—show what it isn't like, use lots of details.*

"What do you think about *paragraphing*," I ask them. "Can the piece be all one unified paragraph, like your profile, or are there any reasons why you'd want more?"

Nobody seems to have an idea. "Well, some of you said you might want to show contrasts—zone versus non-zone."

"Oh yeah," Garret says. "You mean we could make different paragraphs for zone and non-zone?"

"If you think it will help your reader. Or if it feels and looks right, as you read it aloud. I often change my paragraphing as I read aloud, both as I'm drafting and as I revise later on. Ursula Le Guin, the fantasy writer I mentioned earlier—remember, I read you a bit about long paragraphs being okay, from her book on writing, *Steering the Craft?*—she also talks about paragraphing as part of the "architecture" of a piece, not random indents, but important divisions that show the connections and separations in the flow, part of the longer rhythm of the piece, just as sentence lengths create the shorter rhythms. Is there any advantage to keeping your zone piece all one paragraph?"

Peter suggests that if you're writing about "flow," maybe you shouldn't break it up into sections. "But maybe you could write the non-zone in a different font, or italics or something."

"Cool," says Garret, who, I've discovered, loves putting words in huge capitals with lots of exclamation points and green ink.

Sound and Sense

I bring up the question of *rhythm*: first, how a paragraph break creates a silence that you can hear if you listen to your writing. It's important to keep reading the draft aloud, *slowly*. Then there's the choice of short sentences versus longer sentences, and the related question of word sounds—abrupt, staccato words versus smooth, legato words with, say, some long vowels. And I introduce a few other new categories for sounds: nasals (*m, n*), liquids (*l, r*), and sibilants (*s, sh, z, zh*). These will come in useful for poetry, also.

"You mean we should actually try to think about finding words with *l* and *r* to show time kind of flowing along?" asks Julia.

"Well, you may find if you're describing how a conscious, hard, sweaty struggle on a math test gradually becomes a smooth, trouble-free, cruising zone experience of solving the problems, that you're using smoother-sounding words without even trying. This happens to me, especially in writing poems. But you might also find, as you read some of your draft aloud, that your zone sounds too staccato and you want to use some different sounds. Writing is a really interesting mix of conscious and unconscious mind work. Suppose you wanted to create a sense of something being hard at first, a real struggle. What could you do, as a writer?"

There's a long silence. I try again. "Well, can you remember when you first learned to write with a pencil, and you made a letter *H*, say, very carefully. How did the pencil feel in your hand?"

"Oh yeah," says Brooks, "I held the pencil really tight, and my lines weren't straight, so I'd erase them and do it over. I hated writing. It took so long just to do one word."

Jenna's face lights up. "Oh, you could write little, kind of jerky fragments for the not-zone part, and short words that sound—what's that word for it that sounds like what it means?"

"Great, Jenna. Yes, this piece may be a chance to make fragments and run-ons work for you. To break some 'rules.' I'll have to show you all Tom Romano's chapter on 'Breaking the Rules in Style' [*Crafting Authentic Voice*, 77–86]. If you want to test whether your contrast in sentence lengths will register on your reader, what can you do? Right, read aloud. Test it on yourself. You could also try counting words." I tell them it's been said that our ears can't really hear sentence length differences of fewer than four words (Dean, 153). I promise myself we'll try a few of Le Guin's exercises as a mini-lesson once students are ready to revise: "Write a half-page to a page of narrative, up to 350 words, which is all one sentence." And "Write a paragraph of narrative, 100–150 words, in sentences of seven or fewer words. No sentence fragments! Each must have a subject and a verb" (47–48).

"Oh, and the term you wanted, Jenna, is *onomatopoeia*." I write it on the board. Next to it I write *grunt, scratch, jerk, clutch, clunk*. "Anyone want to give us some words that sound smoother, more zone-like? Way to go, Brooks, Sydney, Julia." And I write *loose, glide, breathe,* and *silver*.

Model: Eudora Welty

"And speaking of sounds and comparisons and being in the zone reminds me of a wonderful writer named Eudora Welty, famous for her short stories—she won the Pulitzer Prize years ago—who wrote a brief memoir, *One Writer's Beginnings*. She talks about how, when she was around six years old, she first became physically aware of the roundness of the moon because her different senses suddenly all gave her the same message at the same time: she sees the full moon, just risen, right after sunset, start to fill with light and go, she says, from flat to round, and the word *moon* comes into her mouth—I remember, she says it's as though the word is fed to her out of a silver spoon—and as she holds the word *moon* in her mouth, she feels it has the same roundness as a Concord grape (those deep purple ones) her grandfather picked and gave her to suck out of its skin and swallow whole. She mentions this happened in *Ohio*. I love how Welty's sight and taste and hearing all work together to make her understand roundness, and then how all these *o* sounds, in *Ohio* and in *spoon, moon, whole,* and *swallow* help us feel the roundness, too. My guess is that some of those sounds were conscious choices as she re-created this moment, and some just 'happened.' I'll find the passage and email it to you tonight. I think she must have been in the writing zone when she wrote it.

"I'll post all these suggestions of ours tonight, as part of the directions, the goals, for the piece. Then, when you're ready to revise, these can become the criteria. We'll use them in assessing the draft you turn in, too."

That night, I email them the assignment in Figure 2.6. I make up a list, based on our discussion and this description of the assignment, which each student can check off and turn in with the first draft and revision, and which I can use in conferences as we assess the piece together.

The Writing Mentors

A couple of days later, when the rough drafts are due, I bring in two twelfth-grade mentors from the school Writing Center to visit and give a sample workshop on revising. The ninth graders need to meet a few older students who care about writing. And they need to get an idea of what will happen when they make an appointment with the Writing Center. I've invited one male and one female mentor and sent a copy of our zone assignment to them. (In all my courses, I email my writing assignments to the center so the staff will be prepared if students turn up.) I've asked our two guests to talk briefly about why they applied to become mentors, and what kinds of writing they like to do best. Jeremy is coeditor of the school newspaper, and Caitlyn is a peer group leader for the ninth grade. Both were strong applicants—effective writers whom the English department had found to be confident leaders in class discussions but also good listeners and focused, insightful peer editors. The twenty mentors, juniors and seniors, take turns staffing the center in pairs and generally can each fit two twenty-minute

Think of an occasion—a specific place and time—when you were "at your best" or "in the zone." It's that feeling of being in the right place at the right time with all that you need in order to do what needs to be done. The feeling might come while you're dancing, playing an instrument, working on a project for school, playing a sport, building a website, making an iMovie, going out for a bike ride. . . . What were you feeling? What conditions and circumstances do you think made it possible for you to have this "zone" experience?

Focus on the details and start "in the middle of things" (*in medias res*). The aim is to evoke the feeling of being in the zone, not to narrate a long story. (That is, sometimes being in the zone happens in quiet moments of practice, not in the big game or the recital, and even then it's not about whether you won or not.)

Let the details flow onto the page: where you were, what you were doing and feeling, what was happening around you, the way time was moving or not moving. Don't focus on explaining, but instead stay focused on the sensory details—sounds, smells, what your body and mind were experiencing, feeling.

You may need to make some comparisons—similes, metaphors—to help us get into your skin, walk in your shoes, enter your experience.

Sometimes it helps to note what the experience was NOT like—to draw a contrast. Remember a major contrast can be between non-zone and zone—and that the sounds of words, the rhythm/lengths/types of sentences, paragraphing, even shifts in fonts, can help you create the contrasts.

Shoot for about a page, typed double-spaced. Use as many paragraphs as you need to put us fully into your zone experience.

FIGURE 2.6. ASSIGNMENT FOR "IN THE ZONE."

conferences into a class period. Students in any of the four grades can sign up, on their own or at a teacher's recommendation, to work on a piece for any department, at any stage in the writing process. Students take their own notes during the session, and at the end the mentor fills out and files a form, which the teacher can consult if she or he wishes. The mentor also emails teachers to let them know a student has had a conference. Every

couple of weeks, all mentors meet during lunch with the two English teachers who direct the center, to troubleshoot and to share some good writing
talk.

For this second assignment of the term, I don't want these young students to assess one another's pieces but to watch an older, more experienced
student respond to their writing. Our visitors will choose one brave volunteer and conduct a sample conference on his or her current draft of the
zone piece. Then we'll break into two circles, and while all the ninth graders listen and take notes, each mentor will hear as many students' drafts
aloud as time permits, ask a few questions, and offer some feedback. Those
students who don't get feedback should be able to apply some of the advice
they hear and note down from their peers' conferences. Some kids will be
more interested in the seniors' advice than in mine. Of course, many will
come in hoping that maybe, maybe, their paper is *all done*. But while the
mentors will find things to admire, part of this admiration will consist of
questions and of exhortations to make this fine, promising piece even better.
I will take turns sitting in on the two circles, interrupting only when I think
the students aren't jotting down, or maybe not "getting," a key point.

It's important for the class to understand that the center isn't just for
ninth graders—that even seniors visit it for feedback. A couple of days earlier, I'd had an email exchange with one of the mentors whom I'd taught the
year before in my poetry course. I told him I wanted to introduce my ninth
graders to the Writing Center and wondered whether he might have had an
experience in a conference that he'd like me to pass on to them. He wrote
back:

> It is interesting that you asked about the Writing Center, because I just had
> a rewarding experience working with one of my friends, a senior, on his
> writing. He came to me with a question about one of his short stories; he
> had asked other people to read it, but they had a difficult time understand-
> ing what he was trying to communicate. I read it once, and was confused
> by it, but on the second read I began to realize that it possessed the same
> eerie quality of Ray Bradbury's book *The Martian Chronicles*. I talked with
> him for some time about what had struck me in his story, and how he
> could expand on it; I had also told him how it reminded me of some of the
> science fiction I had read, and I began to identify what aspects of the story
> were particularly effective to me. After we had finished, he felt better, more

confident, and he was looking at his own writing through a new perspective. I had not touched his paper in terms of grammar, or spelling, or any of the mechanics, but instead I provided him with what he really needed: a new frame of mind that he could use to work with his paper. I found that I had also learned something about my own love of science fiction, and I was able to begin to articulate what it was that caught my imagination in some of Bradbury's or Asimov's works that his paper brought me back to. What the Writing Center strives to achieve reminds me of what an artist will tell you to consider as you begin to learn how to draw, or to paint: the first step is not to learn technique, but instead to learn how to see in a new way—like an artist. I think that the Writing Center is a safe place where students can come and learn how to "see" writing in a new way, and the learning is invariably mutual.

Ellis Ratner, grade 12, writing mentor

I think I'll email this to the students tonight after our two mentors' visit so they can hear one more voice, one more perspective, on—well, on so many things that are important to the writing process and the reading–writing connection: the value of "a second read" (for both writer and responder); the advantage of the writer getting a fresh perspective from a sympathetic reader who can start off with what strikes him about the piece, what's already good that could be expanded on; the usefulness of looking at the question of genre, of relating the piece to published work of a similar kind and, perhaps, by an author familiar to the student writer; the connection between creating visual art and writing; the Writing Center as a "safe place"; and, above all, the "mutuality" of the learning that can go on between writer and responder.

Jeremy and Caitlyn introduce themselves. Two of my students, James and Connor, are already interested in writing for the newspaper, so they're glad to meet Jeremy. Several students are in Caitlyn's peer group section and give her a big smile. The rest look nervous. The seniors explain a few things about the center: its purpose is "to empower the writer, to help students gain confidence in their own writing and revising skills. It's not a paper-editing plant nor a place just for students who have writing problems. Even the strongest writers benefit from a visit to the Writing Center." The mentors don't mark up student work and don't correct mechanics, though they may refer a student to a particular section of the all-school writing manual, Diana Hacker's *A Writer's Reference*. Writers are expected to take their own notes on their drafts during the conference.

"And," I add, "I'll read these notes when I read the draft and the revision, to see what use you were able to make of them in the revising process."

Jeremy reads aloud from the center's mission statement: "Student Mentors are, above all, good listeners and responsive readers. They are experienced and committed writers who care about the craft of writing and enjoy the challenge of helping other students discover what they have to say. The best Mentor is the one who can listen with sensitivity and ask the right questions about a student's paper." Caitlyn explains that if a student just wants to run some ideas by the mentor, say for a thesis or a character, that's fine; the mentor can ask clarifying questions. If students come with rough drafts, they'll be asked to read the draft aloud, specify what aspects they want a response to, and then explore these with the mentor.

Conferences with the Mentors

My ninth graders are looking a little anxious. I sense they're wondering, "Suppose I have no idea what to ask? Suppose it's just, like, half a page too short?" So I ask, "What did you folks find was hard when you were making these drafts?" Hands go up.

"I wrote about skating in a competition, but I had so many details, and I didn't know which ones to keep because it was way too long and kind of rambled," Jess offers.

Peter says, "My zone experience happened quite a while ago and it was hard to remember it all."

"I wanted to keep it all one paragraph, but it was hard to make it all flow together," says Connor. "There's some stuff in the middle that I can't make fit."

Julia wonders whether hers is too much just describing a place and not enough "in the zone."

"Why don't you read yours aloud, Julia, and maybe Caitlyn and Jeremy can give you some feedback on that issue," I suggest. I know she's a confident performer; she had a lead in the school's eighth-grade musical last year, and she's been participating a lot in class discussions. I don't think she'll feel nervous.

"Okay. It's called 'The Streets of Spain.' It's kind of short so far." And Julia reads. Meanwhile, Caitlyn's taking notes. At the end, Caitlyn says, "I think you're exactly right. It needs more 'zone.' Some of those details are really strong as description of the place but not necessarily of your zone sensations. You'll need to make some cuts and additions. One thing—all those smells! You've got the positives, the ones you suck in your breath for—pizza, salt from the ocean, night breeze—and you also have Vespa exhaust, but it's 'spreading like a disease through the air.' If that smell is meant to be part of the 'zone' experience, I wonder if you want the image of disease? Well, maybe. . . . And one other thing I noticed, just listening: there's a long sentence in the middle somewhere that had good sounds but didn't make sense to me. Show me the draft? Mmmmm. Yeah, right here: 'Our mouths ate up the silence as we walked home that night, stopping to admire the smallest idea, even though our bodies had moved on.' The length isn't a problem. It's just unclear, the mix of physical and mental or something. The long sentence farther down, though, is really cool, the way it builds and builds very smoothly like it's an experience that will never end—and then it does end just where the sentence does. So cool! Can I read it aloud again? And the real short sentence that leads into it, too: 'But we never stopped laughing. Laughing as we shared stories, as we smelled the sweet salt of the ocean, as the breeze of the night stroked our hair, as we ate ice cream cones, as we zippered our sweaters, laughing as we realized this moment would leave us.' All those 'as' moments piling up like it's one endless moment. I think you guys talked in class with Ms. Michaels about contrasting sentence lengths, didn't you? About trying long, flowing ones for the zone? And short ones for contrast, when you're not in the zone? It's in your list of criteria. So you've done really well with that sentence."

Julia is beaming. "Thanks so much," she says. "I'll work on the disease part. I'm not sure what I meant there. But I want to keep the Vespa exhaust because it was part of the feeling—I could just cut the disease, maybe." She's already revising in her head. And later, when she hands in the new draft, I'll see that she's changed her confusing sentence to read: "Our mouths ate up the silence as we walked home that night; we were relaxed, as if we had no backbone." The mix of taste and hearing—eating the silence—seems to be connected to the loose, relaxed-all-over feeling of having no backbone. It's starting to make more sense. Interesting that in working to clarify, she's also breaking the sentence into two, getting rid of the vaguely attached participle and using a semicolon—correctly. I don't know whether she realizes that her semicolon is helping us connect the mouths eating silence with the sensation of being relaxed, and that it creates a rhythm different from that of the earlier version, but we can talk about this in conference. She adds a sentence about the freedom she felt in this new environment, as well as another, a bit marred by cliché but clearly trying to capture "zone": "It felt like at that very moment, with all senses tingling but yet so at ease, you were standing at the top of the world." A writer is at work here.

The students seem to have calmed down, seeing that Julia has survived her ordeal. I herd them into two circles, one mentor for each. I remind everyone to open writer's notebooks and listen hard so they can jot down questions and suggestions. I remind them that these pieces are *theirs*, that the mentors will honor this and not dictate corrections. "You don't have to take their advice, but Julia seems to have found it useful, and even if you don't get to read your piece, you'll probably hear some ideas that you can apply to it. Just use your imagination."

I disappear for a few minutes to let the seniors take charge, and when I return, James is writing notes on his draft: he's scrawled "focus" up at the top and "unnecessary? plunge in" next to his opening sentence; "cliché—say it differently?" beside "crystal clear"; "switch around?" next to two sentences, with an arrow; "could put first" farther down the page; and "good" over his two closing sentences. Back in the other circle, Caitlyn's saying gently to Hunt, who's written about starring in the eighth-grade musical, *Damn Yankees*, "It's a good overview, I think. Do you have any questions?"

"Not really," he says politely.

"Okay. Well, I think you might try picking out just *one* scene and going into a lot of detail about it as a zone experience. You've tried to cover so many scenes that it ends up being pretty general. One scene—and it could be really intense." Hunt nods but doesn't write down anything. I jog his elbow, smile, mouth "MAKE NOTES," and he strikes his forehead dramatically and opens his laptop.

Garret calls me over to the other circle and whispers, "Hey, I didn't have a draft, I just couldn't think of anything, but Jeremy helped me get a topic. I told him how I love surfing, and he started asking me questions, so I have an idea how I want to start." Why on earth didn't Garret let me know two days ago that he was having a problem? Did he think I'd get mad? Or maybe I just wouldn't notice when his paper didn't come in? But now he's made some notes and he looks excited. It's probably good for him—this small, young-for-his-grade boy—to have a senior guy taking him seriously.

Ayana's asking Jeremy how she can cut back on her descriptions and keep the piece concentrated on her feelings about finally seeing this building she used to draw again and again as a child—the Eiffel Tower.

"I think you need to keep the details that make us *feel* your emotions and cut some of the others that just *tell* us the emotions. For instance, do you need to *tell* us the tower is "an amazing sight that would change my life forever" when you've just *shown* how all the traffic and bustle and even the pinch of your high heels have suddenly stopped and 'a rare quietness' engulfs you—as you see this thing you'd been dreaming of for so long? And then you *show* us how it looks—'magical, glittering and shimmering from the blue lights wrapped around its hard metal frame in the pure darkness of the night.' That's really beautiful. It's the showing with those details, not the telling, that works best."

A couple of other students in the circle are nodding. They smile encouragingly at Ayana. Jeremy and Caitlin's engagement with these pieces has set a tone that apparently makes it okay to take word choice seriously. Nobody's giggling or nudging or even just drifting. As the seniors get ready to leave, Caitlin says, "I've been going through this revising with my college essay. I'm only allowed 500 words, so I'm making cuts and trying to get more humor and energy into it. When I do a first draft, I like to just put down everything that comes to me, but then I have to start cutting. Like, for this essay, I can't cover a whole, long summer experience. I have to pick specific moments in order to make my point." And Jeremy says, "Yeah, I'm learning stuff from writing my college aps, but I think my writing's improved most from being in the Writing Center. It's like peer editing. You learn to figure out what would make somebody else's piece better—how to help them—and then it gets easier to do that for your own papers."

"No, I did *not* coach him to say that. But he's right. Now, how many of you have ideas for changes you want to make?" I ask, as the door closes. Most hands go up. "In addition to trying out these ideas, what else might you do to help make your piece stronger? Yes, read it over aloud, *slowly*, listening to the sounds of words, the rhythms, the lengths of sentences. Imagine you're composing music. And you can also go back to our list of criteria. Pretend you're someone reading the piece who's not had this zone experience: Where is the piece successfully putting you *into* the experience?

Where is it just giving information about a place or event, as if it were a report? Reading aloud, by the way, can also help you hear where the punctuation isn't working or where a sentence needs more glue—or a different kind of glue, in a different place."

"Are we going to make a collection of these for everyone?" Nick asks. "Like with the profiles?"

"Yeah, let's," says Garret, who hasn't written his yet. "But give us more time in class to read everybody's. And maybe cupcakes?"

So Far/What Next?

Teaching writing can make you dizzy. You need to focus on the present task, but at the same time you're trying to take stock of the past week and looking ahead to the next one. What have these kids learned that they can build on? The next item on the agenda is discussing and writing about their summer book, *Catcher in the Rye*. What kind of writing might enlarge their repertoire of genres and skills for the free-choice project a couple of months from now but also offer a fair assessment of their reading and the discussions we'll have of *Catcher*?

With the help of the writing mentors, students are, I think, recognizing that revision is a natural part of writing, not a requirement peculiar to one teacher but something that may continue to be useful to them, even as seniors. And, from Jeremy, that responding helpfully to another person's writing can help you improve your own. These attitudes help to create a sense of being a community of writers. At least some of the kids are starting to internalize certain writing values:

1. A good lead and a strong conclusion matter; just stating a piece's topic at the outset or summarizing at the end doesn't cut it.

2. Structuring a piece is tricky business, often a matter of trial and error.

3. Developing a paragraph with specific sensory details or quotations or examples makes it more alive, more fun to read, more memorable.

4. Voice has something to do with "attitude" and with words, and we don't all have to sound alike.

We could spend more time on the zone piece. But if students just work on eliminating the old mistakes, they'll never get to make new ones. And they'll rapidly lose interest in writing. The journey toward proficiency—my own included—is full of switchbacks. Rather than getting mired in repeated drills and revisions, these restless teens need to move ahead to a new challenge, even if *that* challenge doesn't produce total success either. After all, Holden Caulfield tells us that one has to let kids risk a fall from the goddam carrousel horse if they want to grab for the gold ring.

Chapter 3

Becoming Holden: Writing Narrative— Fact and Fiction

A Day in the Life of Holden Caulfield

We were on our way to the Princeton battlefield. There was some famous battle fought there or something. My bus was full of phonies. It really was. There was some guy with some girl in the seat behind me. I didn't have anything better to do, so I listened in on their conversation. The guy was a real moron. He kept telling the girl that she should let him take her out, but she kept reminding him that they had just met a week ago. The world would be so much better if there wasn't always some guy asking some girl out. But there was this girl in the seat next to me, she was quite attractive, so I leaned over and said, "How's it going?" suave as hell.

She said, "Pretty good. How about yourself?"

"I'm swell." Then all of a sudden I couldn't help myself. "Did ya ever notice how many phonies we've got in this school?" I asked her.

"Excuse me?" she said.

"You know, the type of people who always run to get to the back of the bus."

"I'm not so sure I know what you mean," replied the girl in this maddening voice.

"Forget about it," I said. There was no point in trying to have an intelligent conversation with her. I was actually glad when we got to the field and they split us up into our six groups.

The first thing our group leaders made us do was partner up with somebody and we had to learn two new things about the person. My partner
wasn't bad or anything. It's just that when he started talking he wouldn't
stop. He kept telling me about how he got to go to Europe and got to join a
summer school program in England. His name was Xavier. I didn't bother
to ask his last name. It didn't seem very important. Anyway, old Xavier
kept telling me about this girl he met in England and how he and this girl
would neck all the time. He said he almost gave her the time at a party
once. He probably wasn't telling the truth. He probably even made up the
part about meeting the girl. I wasn't really paying much attention. After old
Xavier finished babbling about England, we had to share what we learned
about our partner with the whole group. Fortunately before it was my turn
the teachers said it was time to start playing kickball.

I told my group leaders that I had to go to the bathroom before the game
started. I didn't really have to, but I wasn't feeling too well, if you want to
know. What I did do was light a cigarette, though. I knew it would be okay
because everyone would be playing kickball. They wouldn't miss that for
the world. While I was smoking my cigarette, I started wondering if anybody would miss me if I were to leave right now, if I got up and walked into
the woods and never came back. Sure they'd come looking for me once
they realized I was gone, but how long would that take? Right then I started
to think about old Phoebe. She would have come looking for me for sure.
Boy she would have loved to be here playing kickball, meeting guys that
won't stop talking about England, and talking about her feelings. I figured
I'd at least try to have fun for her. I wish I could have traded places with
her. Phoebe doesn't mind school too much. She can have fun anywhere, it
doesn't matter what she's doing.

I finished my cigarette and headed back to where my group was playing
kickball. When I got there I told them I couldn't play because I had a knee
condition. It made me depressed watching all of my classmates having
so much fun just by kicking a goddamn ball. I almost wanted to join, but
I was never really the athletic type of guy. Once I started thinking about
myself playing I got even more depressed. I don't know why, but everything seemed so damn depressing all of a sudden. Anyway the day went on
with all these dumb activities they made us do. There was this one activity
where a person picked a question and everyone had to go around in a circle
and answer it. I came up with some terrific lie every time it was my turn to
answer a question. I think Phoebe would have liked making up stuff.

The day ended with each group putting on a skit using props that were
in a garbage bag. I thought that this might actually be a little bit of fun. I

figured at least I'd get to watch all the morons make fools of themselves when it was their turn. I let the rest of my group argue about what we were going to do for our skit. I just did what they told me to do. There was this one kid who actually had quite a bit of talent. He had everyone, even the teachers, laughing the entire time. I thought this guy might actually be somewhat fun to shoot the bull with, but I didn't think I'd talk to him. You really have to be in the mood to do that sort of stuff with someone you never met before, and anyway, I still wasn't feeling very well.

Finally we got back on the buses. I sat in the very front, as far away from the phonies as possible. On the way back to school we passed a park and I saw a man playing catch with his son. It reminded me of Allie, D.B., and I all playing catch in the park. D.B. was the only one that was any good, but we still had fun. Allie's mitt sure was something, with the poems in green ink and all. The next thing I knew, everyone was brushing past me to get off the bus. I must have fallen asleep. Then I wondered if I really did see that kid playing catch with his dad. Probably not. I really am a madman.

Brooks Backinoff, grade 9

Brooks's Preliminary Lists (collected from annotations and class discussions)
Holdenisms
>   and all
>   lousy
>   sonuvabitch
>   it kills me
>   helluva
>   it knocks me out
>   phonies
>   as hell
>   necking
>   like a madman
>   he really did, you really would
>   pimply
>   made me sore
>   swell
>   if you know what I mean
>   moron
>   you would have puked
>   boy, you really should have been there
>   I don't even want to talk about it

Topics Holden Often Digresses To
> the ducks in Central Park
> Jane
> Allie
> Phoebe
> Sally Hayes
> the movies
> stories from his three old schools
> phonies (kids, teachers)
> future plans

Commentary

Up until this third writing assignment, Brooks had focused entirely on base-ball, both in his profile of Matt and his zone piece. A frustrated ballplayer, out all season due to an injury the previous spring, he'd made it clear during our first conference that he liked his stories action-packed; they should move straight to a climax with no unnecessary descriptions or pauses for thought. Holden Caulfield's long digressions and frequent mood shifts annoyed him. My requests for annotating and reflecting also annoyed him. In filling out his introduction sheet the first day of class, he wrote that his favorite types of assignments were "the ones where you don't have to do anything." But somehow Brooks managed to enter the mind of J. D. Salinger's Holden and inhabit it long enough to write four pages of narrative, imagining how this guy—so seemingly different from himself—might have reacted to our school's ninth-grade peer group retreat. I think it was this assignment that helped him the most when it came to writing his free-choice project, a ten-page story—convincingly detailed and developed in part through interior monologue—about a high school ballplayer who becomes dependent on steroids and dies in a car crash that may or may not be suicide. In an end-of-the-year assessment, Brooks reflected: "I love being able to do whatever I want, just be totally creative and change my plot whenever I want," but "I've found I can also be creative in writing 'guideline' assignments, where I have to stick to one given subject or analyze a certain book or speech or theme. I worry less now when I have to follow guidelines." In synthesizing his writing experiences, he concluded that poems, essays, and stories all need "good description or good textual evidence—specifics that make things real"—and that "they all need a focus." These discoveries reveal a student progressing on the journey toward—and beyond—writing proficiency.

What's most striking about his Holden piece is that Brooks isn't simply plugging in phrases from a list of expressions to imitate Holden's voice but is actually taking on a way of thinking and a psyche that felt foreign to him. Brooks's work demonstrates the difference between imitation and transformation. I'm wondering what bridge Salinger's novel offers that helped Brooks's imagination enter a mind so seemingly unlike his own, a mind that couldn't, or wouldn't, tell a straight story and swung, sometimes wildly, between trust and alienation, delight and suicidal despair. What enabled him to connect with another, to achieve what Katherine Paterson says is our fundamental task as human beings? I think the bridge may be Holden's teenage oscillating between child and adult—ironically, the root of that very ambivalence so irritating to Brooks. Even those students who are least sympathetic to Holden and most resistant to ambivalence can cross that particular bridge.

Reading and Rereading the Text

Our department assigns *Catcher in the Rye* to the incoming ninth graders both as the required summer reading and as the opening book of the ninth-grade year. In June we post on the school's summer reading site, along with suggested and required books, some directives for "active reading" that we hope will lay groundwork for the reading and writing community we try to create in our classrooms. These establish the journey archetype as a theme for the grade 9 year and point out that books written several thousand years apart may explore similar questions and present similar human characteristics. They point out that a story or journey consists not only of a chain of events but also of encounters between people, and they ask the students to write some notes on whichever of Holden's encounters interest and/or puzzle them. The directives invite students to be open to the coexistence of opposites within a work of art—for instance, a character who's both "real" and created, both strong and weak, both funny and troubled, whose journey is both literal and figurative and who wants but doesn't want to find his way home. The awareness of tensions such as these, which lie at the heart of *Catcher* and many other books, can help make the ninth graders' reading, discussions, and writing stronger. We also post a few open-ended discussion questions, the kind we want students to learn to ask of themselves and of one another.

In class this year I start the *rereading* process with an assignment I've cribbed from David, our department chair (see Figure 3.1). I like it because it honors the students' initial reading back in the summer but makes a good case for the value of rereading. I like that it makes some clear connections between the book and the students' own experiences, and between reading and writing. And I find it a good way to introduce the concept of "having a dialogue with a text."

1. **Reread** Chapters 1 and 2.

2. **Annotating in book and/or notebook**: Now that you know Holden's story and have formed some opinion of his character, what details do you notice in your second reading that *either confirm or make you reconsider* your feelings about him? What questions left after your first reading are you looking to answer? What new questions does your second reading raise? A creative reader engages in a *dialogue with the text*, testing her thoughts and feelings against the details, and the dialogue is richer the second time around because you notice more of the details and have a better sense of their significance.

3. What do we mean by "significant detail"? Think of your own life. Think of some little thing that might not mean much to strangers but that says a lot about you. All you have to do is mention it and your friends or family will nod their heads knowingly. **In your writer's notebook, write a paragraph describing** that little thing. **Tell a little story** that shows how it fits into your life. Show what it says about you, how and why it is a "significant detail" in your story.

FIGURE 3.1. COMING BACK TO CATCHER IN THE RYE.

Rethinking My Writing Assignment on Catcher in the Rye

When I first taught *Catcher*, I used it as a vehicle for introducing the writing of an analytical essay—this despite the fact that the department presented it as a story and invited students to respond to it as the adventures of a teenage journey. What a natural opportunity for students to try their hand at writing narrative! But no, that hadn't occurred to me. Each year the essays ranged from a couple of thoughtful, well-developed pieces by kids who were clearly born to be English majors, to a large quantity of bland, unfocused, and sometimes plagiarized papers, full of inaccurate plot summaries. I tried breaking the assignment down into steps: annotations, quickwrites, drafts, peer edits, revisions; I provided some models; I demonstrated my own writing process. No good. Finally this summer a colleague suggested that perhaps *storytelling* is a more natural form for young teens than the analytical essay, especially when they're coming off two months of summer vacation.

With that suggestion and the free-choice project in mind, I began to wonder whether my students might be able to write a narrative in Holden's voice. We'd always had fun collecting Holden's expressions, initially for the thrill of swearing in class but also for the opportunities to look into the ways slang and colloquialisms change over time. I had discovered the preface to the *Random House Webster's Dictionary*, "Defining Our Language for the 21st Century," which listed new words by the decade when they'd first appeared, starting with the 1940s, Holden's period. Using these lists, we'd imagined how a Holden from each decade might sound, right up to the present, when the students became the experts. Their interest had led me to assign some brief writing in Holden's voice, which the class enjoyed doing and sharing but which soon struck me as superficial—an imitation, a game of plugging in words rather than an imaginative transformation. What would it take to "become Holden," not just use his vocabulary? What new writing challenges would arise, and would these flow naturally from our two previous pieces— the profile and "in the zone"? Certainly the narrative would need a larger framework than we'd been using in the voice exercise.

Okay, storytelling. Holden needed to tell a new story. Maybe he could narrate a series of encounters and actions based on some event that my students had recently experienced, so they wouldn't have to invent the whole framework. What events did most of our ninth graders experience together early in the fall? Peer group retreat; Community Service Day; Homecoming Weekend. Whichever event they chose, they'd have to imagine from Holden's perspective—that of a critical, idealistic, depressed, self-mocking adolescent. And in his own rhythms, digressions and all. The piece would be, in some ways, a more demanding—and for many students a more interesting—assignment than the old analytical essay. Would it be a fair and revealing assessment of their reading and writing abilities? How well could they capture Holden's complexity?

And what skills from their profiles and zone pieces could students apply to this new challenge? Well, from the profile: their use of quotation and descriptions of gesture and facial expression; the combining of their subject's voice with their own reflections; the organizing of their subject's experience (the activity, memory, or snapshot) by marking shifts in time through strategic transitions and verb tense; and the exploration of some tension or contrasts within the focused topic. From the zone piece: the creation, in first person, of contrasting physical and mental states—conscious, effortful struggle versus the effortless "flow"—through sensory details and imagery, through sound and sentence rhythm; and, as in the profile, the combining of narration, description, and reflection.

What would be new? Adapting a complex persona—"becoming" Holden; narrating a series of events in that persona's language and rhythms; inventing Holden-like digressions to reflect his obsessions with particular people, his fears and loves; and creating natural transitions between the digressions and the narrative episodes. Plenty of writing challenges.

Students Teaching

I realized that I was now viewing the rereading of *Catcher* not simply as our initial exploring of the journey archetype, or the study of a teenager struggling with growing up, or the analysis of a modern classic novel, but also as a means of expanding my students' initiative and range *as writers*. To help the class succeed in this complicated writing assignment—and make it not only a fair assessment of their study of the novel but also a helpful preparation for the free-choice writing project a couple of months from now—I would need to focus a lot of class time on "reading as a writer." Students would need to take ownership of the book in the way that our department had asked in the summer posting about active reading: relate to Holden as if he were real but keep in mind that he is a voice created by Salinger. Somehow I would need to balance class discussions of the book with writing workshops and try to make sure that each operation fed and was nourished by the other.

Since we were rereading the book and it was our first book of the year, I thought this was the perfect opportunity, in the name of "taking owner-ship" of *Catcher* as readers and writers, to ask students to direct the discus-sions. For a couple of years now, I'd assigned pairs of students to lead the class through a cluster of three chapters, but I'd gotten more and more bright ideas about what purposes these lesson plans should serve in the fifty available minutes: in the name of diversified learning styles and multiple intelligences, writing as inquiry, writing as genre study, collaborative learn-ing, multicultural literacy, gender differences, and creative use of technol-ogy, things had gotten a trifle out of hand. Moreover, this early in the year ninth graders really weren't ready to handle so much responsibility, either as teachers or as cooperative learners. Supervising notebook quickwrites, small-group discussions, and role-playing games; presenting a video or au-dio clip; writing on the board while keeping their peers focused; and leading an effective wrap-up—I couldn't have juggled all this myself!

But creating a workable *lesson plan*, especially if the student pairs could focus it on writing and on reading as writers—maybe providing writing prompts—would be valuable, even if the planners didn't actually conduct the class session themselves. I could return to my role as class facilitator but honor the teaching pairs by following their lesson plan. They could post it to the online class conference the night before, so we could all review the chapters and consider the prompts that night. Because I wanted everyone to have some preparation in common, I asked—as I'd always done with *Catcher*—that we all write our own titles for the three chapters (Salinger provides no titles—a good issue to discuss); list three or four key events for each chapter; mark with an *H* and an annotation a few passages that shed new light on Holden; and choose one passage from each chapter that might be good to explore next day in class.

Creating the Template for Student Lesson Plans

I stripped down my grandiose template to more reasonable proportions, keeping in mind the year's theme of physical and psychological journey, as well as the free-choice project ahead. I started with a required summary: each pair would provide a list of the various places Holden goes in these three chapters; the new characters he encounters and their connections to his life and possible significance to his journey; and a few inferences that might be drawn about Holden's character from some of these encounters. I knew this material would be handy for everyone to have in common during the next day's writing and discussions, as well as later when they started their piece in Holden's voice. The summary and inferences would also help me assess the reading abilities of each student pair. And using the template every day might help the class internalize a pattern they could use as they encountered more books—one way to think about connections between settings, plot, and characterization. One way to read as writers.

For the second section, I asked the student pairs to choose specific passages as prompts for the class to explore in their writer's notebooks and in subsequent discussion. I wanted students to begin to appreciate the value of close reading—of taking us to the text, both in quickwrites and in discussion. They needed, as budding writers, to think about how Salinger creates Holden and his world through specific word choice, imagery, dialogue, and Holden's own reflections (those passages that feel like internal monologues unless we imagine him actually recounting his thoughts and feelings to a therapist). How could I best help my students "watch" Salinger moving between scene and reflection? How could I get them curious about how he handles time? Or ensure that they experience Holden as "both created and real"? They would need all this awareness when they came to write their piece as Holden. So in the template I asked the teaching pairs to list, from anywhere in their three chapters, two passages that struck them as interesting in terms of the writing. Everybody could choose one of these to write about in class the next day. I urged the pair to ask themselves and each other, "What might be lost if this passage were not in the book?" I wasn't asking them to second-guess Salinger here, to answer why he wrote this passage—to commit the intentional fallacy—but rather to consider what impact the passage had on their own experience of the book. (I have participated in aesthetic education workshops at Lincoln Center Institute for many summers and took to heart Maxine Greene's mantra: free yourself to imagine how a work of art, or a life situation, for that matter, "could be otherwise.")

I included in the template my own directive to the class for writing on each prompt: Whichever passage you choose, make sure to explore (1) in what way(s) it's important to the book, based on your reading and rereading, and (2) what personal connections you can make to it—connections with your own experience or something you've read, viewed, heard (which might include a poem or book or news article, a piece of visual art, a movie, a song, etc.) I planned to allot ten minutes for this quickwrite, or longer if students seemed engaged, and then divide the class into two groups according to who chose which passage, give ten minutes for each group to discuss the prompt, and finally bring the groups together for ten or fifteen minutes to see what connections might be made between the two passages, their respective chapters, and previous or future parts of the book.

Last, for section three I asked the pair of students to agree on one broad question, arising from any aspect or issue in their three chapters that they thought would be interesting and fun for the whole class to discuss—that couldn't be answered with "yes" or "no" and that would take us beyond the book. I wanted the class to see the range of "places" a work of art can take us, to what philosophical or ethical speculations a mere "story" can lead a reader. I hoped there would be time left the next day for at least some preliminary discussion of the team's question; perhaps it could spill out into the halls and the lunchroom after class. I resolved to put each new issue up on the wall and leave it there so that before we began the Holden's Voice piece, we'd be able to review all of these questions. I wanted the questions to matter: to register with students each day, at least visually; to remind us of the students who raised them (community building again); and to provide some continuity, not just for this unit but throughout the year. I envisioned this continuity in terms of themes, of ongoing "real life" issues, and of the need to challenge our easy assumptions—to imagine "how things could be otherwise." Maybe the growing list of questions would reflect, too, some growth in the students' ability to articulate thoughtful questions—to think.

In designing the template, I was also thinking about differentiated learning styles and temperaments. The quickwrite would offer practice in close reading for those students who were prone to generalize too much from personal bias or conventional assumptions rather than slow down to consider textual evidence; the subsequent small-group discussion of the prompt would especially benefit those students who lacked confidence in speaking or tended to hold back until they were sure they had something to say; and the broad question, open to the whole class, would allow for freer and more impulsive thinking and a wider frame of reference. Such questions, seemingly less directly rooted in the text, would engage those students who hadn't necessarily loved (or finished?) the book or who liked to argue about "big ideas" or "real life" issues that allowed them to draw on personal experience and convictions, current events, movies, etc. Or who simply enjoy what they called "getting random."

Annotation and Discussion: Taking Us to the Text

I focused discussion of the first two chapters myself, on the required preparations: chapter titles, annotations, and passage choices. I wanted to see who needed help with annotating, who assumed they didn't need to review or annotate at all (since they'd already read the book once), and who found the reading difficult. This was our first class discussion of a book, and I didn't want a pair of students to see their lesson plan go down in flames just because their peers hadn't prepared well. Most of the class had enjoyed creating titles, so we discussed some of the different kinds of titles and the reasons why some appealed to us more than others.

"I don't like the factual ones so much, that tell you what or who," Ayana says. "Like 'The Day I Left Pencey Prep' or 'Old Spencer.' You can figure that out for yourself. They don't add anything."

"They might be useful if you had to review for a test," Sydney offers.

"I liked how Julia used a quote for her title," Conner says. "'I felt like I was disappearing' is a really cool quote, because it kind of foreshadows how, pretty near the end of the story, he's asking Allie, in his head, to keep him from disappearing. At least, once you've read the book you know it's foreshadowing. And even the first time, if you saw that quote at the top of the chapter for the title, you'd probably think twice."

"Julia, could you take us to that page and maybe read the lines right before and right after your quote, to put it in context?" I ask her. "And from here on in, whenever somebody wants to cite or refer to a specific moment in a chapter, it'll help if you give us the page so we can all go there together to see just how that moment works. It'll help you when you come to write your piece in Holden's voice, and with your free-choice piece, too. Kind of like watching a game, if you play that particular sport—you want to see how the team or the player made the point happen. How does Salinger lead into Julia's line and follow up on it?"

Julia takes us to the page. I make her wait until everyone's there with us; it's still that time of year when students don't really believe they have to do this. She reads,

> Anyway, as soon as I got my breath back, I ran across Route 204. It was icy as hell and I damn near fell down. I don't even know what I was running for—I guess I just felt like it. After I got across the road, I felt like I was sort of disappearing. It was that kind of a crazy afternoon, terrifically cold, and no sun out or anything, and you felt like you were disappearing every time you crossed a road. (8)

Julia reads aloud well—another reason I asked her to do this. And the passage can lead us in a lot of useful directions.

"Did Julia do any things in her reading aloud that seemed helpful?" I ask. "Any things you might want to try the next time you read aloud to us?"

"She didn't rush it," Jess notes. "And she kind of made her voice sound like Holden's confused. . . . Maybe it was her pauses or something?"

"It's weird," says Peter thoughtfully, "I didn't notice it when I read it last night, but when I heard it out loud just now, you can hear how Holden's repeating stuff—'across Route 204, crossed a road, felt like it, felt like I was disappearing, you felt like you were disappearing.'"

"Peter, that's something I didn't notice till now either. Anybody else have any thoughts about that?"

"Wow," says Nick, "did he do that on purpose? Uh, Salinger, I mean."

"You know, you could probably answer that as well as I could," I suggest. "Remember when *you* were revising, or even just drafting, say, your profile or your zone piece? Think about moments when you changed a word, maybe cut out a repetition or took out one detail and put in a different one. Did you have a reason—maybe not a totally conscious reason, maybe more like an intuition? For instance, I think one of the poems I'm working on right now wants to sound more jerky, like a scared person trying to think—so I'm making some changes to try to have that happen, including some repetition.

But I didn't *know* I wanted it to move this way till I'd gotten a whole draft done. I think if you read as a writer does, you'll sense how Salinger's repeating helps make Holden's mood seem real—his confusion, maybe this mix of exhilaration and fear now that he's leaving Pencey, this urge to run and the 'craziness' of the day. Why don't you all annotate this passage. Trying to put your thought into words, just a note, can help you figure out what you do think. Writing *is* thinking. What might you write in the margin? Yes, you can underline the repetition that Peter showed us and maybe write "rep," but what could you write so you understand the *effect* of the rep—what it contributes to our sense of Holden? Yes, James?"

"You could write 'rep., H's crazy fear he'll disappear'. Or 'rep., H's obsessing.' Because he's always obsessing about stuff."

"Okay, good. Could anybody imagine obsessing about crossing roads? Does that seem crazy of Holden?" Long silence, or it feels like one. I count slowly to twenty, trying not to answer my own question. Finally a hand goes up. This is not one of those spontaneous discussions where everyone's competing to speak and in too big a hurry to raise hands. It may not qualify as "authentic discussion," that is, motivated by student curiosity. But it's valuable nonetheless. *Authentic* may be one of those value words so powerful that they blind us to other kinds of pedagogical good. My question isn't the students' question, but it's not one that I planned to ask, either; it grew naturally, authentically, from Julia's passage choice and my effort to teach the skill of annotating. I'm suddenly curious . . . roads . . . thresholds? boundaries? . . . what associations might these kids make, if I give them a chance?

"Well," says Jenna, "maybe this is too deep or something, but in fairy tales, bridges are often really dangerous things to get across, and a road could be like a bridge, a test, or—oooh, like Alice moving onto the next square on the chess board. But Holden isn't trying to really get anywhere like become a queen. I don't think he knows what he's doing with his life . . . uh, maybe that's why he feels like he might disappear, kind of lose himself? Because he's scared to go home?"

"Yeah, deep!" says Brooks. "But you can't put all that in a note."

"Well, Jenna?"

"Uh, this is really hard. I guess . . . oh, I could use an equal sign, like put 'rep. of disappear = lose self, going nowhere.'"

"That's really good thinking, Jen. Good condensing. You all need to develop your own shorthand or abbreviations for notes. I think I'll put Jen's note in my book, too. One of the good things about rereading this together is that we can draw on everybody's ideas about the writing and the characters. You can note down other people's ideas if they make sense to you, and they can record yours."

I'm trying to lay groundwork here for the students' own lesson plans and all our future discussions of reading and writing. I'm trying to teach them: Don't be afraid to work from *small* things—one passage, specific words and images; take us to the text for evidence; read aloud, and read *well* to bring the moment to life; listen well, hear something new; distilling a thought into a note is hard but can be clarifying; value and annotate useful comments from classmates; let your own writing experience help you see how the writer is making a character, a speaker or thinker, seem real. And as far as the broad question required by our lesson plan, thinking in *larger* terms—well, Connor's comment about foreshadowing has already suggested a relation between Julia's chapter title, "I felt like I was sort of disappearing," and Holden's emotional journey throughout the book. We can also use this passage to start lists of Holden's vocabulary and speaking patterns, which we'll need for exploring his character and writing in his voice.

Matt's Lesson Plan

I explain to the students how their lesson plans will work, and that our focus on the connections between Holden's *voice* and his *character*—how each creates the other—will prepare them to narrate one of three upcoming grade 9 events from *his* viewpoint. I mention how this experience of narrating a series of events with dialogue and reflection, "becoming" Holden by inhabiting his language, thought patterns, and values, will broaden their writing repertoire as we move toward the free-choice project. Then I assign all my pairs their three chapters.

I'm scheduling a few breaks from this format of write-and-discuss: a day to watch parts of a video about Salinger's life and ask an imaginary Salinger some questions (we can take turns "answering" for him); a day to play a theater game called "Holden's Head," in which one person reads Holden's lines and another is cued to interrupt with what he might actually be feeling (the subtext); and a day to stage, in small groups, a few brief scenes from the book, creating props and sound effects with our own bodies. As I plan the unit, I keep in mind the "Capacities for Imaginative Learning," developed at Lincoln Center Institute. I want to try to engage all these "capacities" in my students—"noticing deeply, questioning, embodying, identifying patterns, making connections, exhibiting empathy, living with ambiguity, creating meaning, taking action, and reflecting/assessing" (5). In working with ninth graders, I particularly want to emphasize embodying: "to experience a work of art or other object of study through your senses, as well as emotionally, and also to physically represent that experience." This must be the one capacity that is most often neglected in high school classrooms. (I mean, how do you measure it?) I can't easily forget the ninth-grade boy who told me a few weeks ago, with shattering frankness, "I just *don't like* sitting and reading and talking and writing for a whole period, Ms. Michaels. I just can't do it." I know this is hard for a lot of us, not only ADHD students— and not just boys either (though the classic male admonition *"Reading Don't Fix No Chevys"* [Smith and Wilhelm] does spring to mind). When I watch my students participate in role-playing games, respond to visuals and music or make their own, become interviewers and reporters, or work in groups to build taxicabs with their bodies, I see certain kids in an entirely new light. Just as important, they have a chance to see themselves and each other differently. Follower may become leader. The "weak" or "slow" English student may suddenly blossom into "gifted and talented."

But first we need to establish the rhythm of preparing and carrying out the students' lesson plans. Since my class isn't made up of an even number of students, I invite Matt to be my partner for our next chapters, 3, 4, and 5. Very quiet in class, maybe because he's new and therefore cautious, but clearly bright and hard-working, Matt has been Brooks's partner in peer editing, but I want to push Brooks into taking more initiative with homework; for the lesson plan, he might rely on Matt's conscientiousness too much. No, I'll put Brooks with a disorganized, unfocused kid and hope his sense of team spirit will take over. I ask Matt if he'd rather we split up the chapters between us or work together, and he decides to split up and then check out each other's work by email. That night I send him my work on Chapter 3, which he approves, and he sends me his work on Chapters 4 and 5. This includes a writing prompt that raises questions about Holden and Jane Gallagher's relationship:

> When Stradlater mentions he is going on a date with Jane, Holden gets ex-
> cited and keeps talking about when she used to live near him two summers
> ago. Do you think he wanted to be strictly friends or more than friends?
> Do you think his feelings have changed at all over the past two years? How
> would you describe their relationship? (40–44)

Matt has taken us to a very long "passage"—four or five whole pages. This probably reflects the fear that many students have of working from a small piece of text: "It won't give me enough to write about." So I email him to ask which part of those pages feels the most significant to him, and he writes that it's the way Jane keeps her kings in the back row when they play checkers because she just likes the way they look all lined up there, and maybe also her "lousy childhood" with "the booze hound stepfather" who ran around the house naked a lot. I suggest maybe he could narrow his pages down to those two paragraphs and still preface them with his questions about Holden's feelings for Jane. I emphasize that this process of choosing passages for prompts is new to everyone and that I think his choice is going to be very useful—and fun—for us to write and talk about, both in connection with the book as a whole and as a window into our own friendships with the opposite sex.

Matt's broad question for whole-class discussion (part three of the template) is excellent, especially because we've just had a school assembly on plagiarism, featuring a dean from the local university. Matt writes: "What exactly is Holden's situation when Stradlater asks him to write the English composition for him? What would you have done if you were Holden in that exact same situation?" He's focused us on the specific situation *first*, asking us to consider Holden at this particular moment. He's also invited us to imagine ourselves as the "enabler" rather than the more usual approach of imagining under what conditions we might copy from someone else. This discussion topic might well increase students' willingness to enter the world of Holden's mind. The details of the situation will seem plausible to many of them, maybe all too familiar. Also, they'll be interested in what their peers think, so even in the whole-class discussion, they'll listen to one another.

Matt's question may also help us talk about Holden's complexity, his ambivalence, an issue that will be important when we start writing from his viewpoint. Holden does sit down to cheat—to write Stradlater's essay that has to be "descriptive as hell" about a room or a house, "something you once lived in or something" (37), but which mustn't be too good, or it won't sound like Stradlater's writing. "That sonuvatbitch Hartzell thinks you're a hot-shot in English, and he knows you're my roommate" (37). We see Holden in his pajamas and red hunting hat, prepared to write in somebody else's voice but "not too crazy about describing rooms and houses" (49)—a topic that has been given him (and probably Stradlater, too) with no context. But then he realizes that his late brother Allie's left-handed fielder's mitt is in his suitcase and that it's "a very descriptive subject" because Allie had written poems in green ink all over the fingers and the pocket "so he'd have some-thing to read when he was in the field and nobody was up at bat" (49). As Holden tells us about Allie, who died of leukemia—"You'd have liked him"—and relives his reactions to his brother's death, it's hard to condemn him for plagiarism. Especially as you sense the essay becoming an authentic expres-sion of his love for Allie, as he copies down the poems from the mitt. "I sort of liked writing about it" (51), he tells us. Holden does change Allie's name so the essay will seem like Stradlater's—so there's clearly some conscious deception—but he admits he "wasn't too crazy about doing it" (51).

When Stradlater comes home later and gets mad at him for writing an unusable essay, off the assigned topic—"No wonder you're flunking the hell out of here. . . .You don't do *one damn thing* the way you're supposed to" (53)—Holden grabs the paper back and tears it up. Some student is sure to say that therefore Holden hasn't participated in plagiarism; the essay hasn't been turned in. But more interesting to me is how even when he seems to accept cheating (in spite his dislike of "phoniness") as a normal part of his school world, and is willing to do it himself, Holden's genuineness takes over; he writes about something that matters to him. My guess is that it's a good essay. Which raises the issue of finding one's own topic versus writ-ing to order. I'm remembering now what Brooks would write, months later, in his self-evaluation—that he'd found he could chart his own way even through an assignment with pretty specific guidelines, make it his own and end up feeling good about the piece.

Using the Student Lesson Plans

Matt and I post our lesson plan online, and next day we carry it out (with five minutes first for independent reading and then a quick share of some chapter titles). The small-group discussions go well; I wander from one group to the other, kibitzing. Sometimes my silent modeling of close attention—making eye contact with whoever's speaking—reminds the kids to do this, too. Occasionally I push them to stick with a point longer, maybe test it against personal experience or consider it in relation to the rest of the book. I make a few notes for myself, on who's confused, who's responding to others' ideas, who's supporting a point well. I peer over kids' shoulders to see how much they were able to write within the time limit. Most agree, when I ask, that they think the preliminary writing helped make the discussions easier and more interesting.

"Maybe I didn't write a whole lot, but thinking over the passage gave me something I wanted to say," Nick offers.

The groups come back together and are able to make some connections between their two topics. Someone suggests that Holden is protective toward anyone who he knows could be hurt, whether it's someone he likes a lot, like Jane, or someone who's really "nasty," like Ackley. Connor, our expert on foreshadowing, says that this foreshadows all the times later in the book when Holden wants to protect younger kids from seeing graffiti. Somebody else sees a connection between Holden's trying to sock Stradlater in the jaw when he thinks Stradlater's "given Jane the time" and his instinct to put his fist through the glass and break lots of windows the night Allie died. And Julia, who's been looking thoughtful, suddenly says that maybe that's why he admires Allie so much for never getting mad at anybody, because Holden's always getting mad at people, even when he says he's being stupid. There's just enough time for the discussion of plagiarism to get going. Indeed, it's still going as kids leave the room. I write Matt's question on the wall in the hope that they'll go on thinking about it. That night the next pair of students posts their plans to the online class conference. During the next four days, we follow each teaching team's lead, rereading, writing chapter titles, and annotating our three chapters in preparation for the next day's quickwrites and discussions. In general, passage choices and questions are good. I just have to remind myself that we won't be "covering" everything I might feel is crucial. These are the students' choices, not necessarily mine. I'm learning what strikes *them* as worth writing and talking about.

For some kids, five to ten minutes of writing produces very brief responses to the prompts, and we agree that writing under a time limit is frustrating. I remind them that the two passage choices *are* posted the night before, so they can review them and do some preliminary thinking ahead of time if they choose to—unlike the procedures for standardized tests. I mention that annotating thoughtfully as they're rereading the book can help them think and write faster in class: they'll have already done some good thinking and put it into words in the margins, and they're getting practice in finding words for their thoughts. Gradually they'll become more fluent on paper. I stress that this is *exploratory* writing; they needn't spend precious time crafting great topic sentences, incorporating quotes gracefully, weighing their word choices, or even reaching a conclusion, though I do require full sentences as a means to clarify thinking. However, after a week of student lessons and writing in class, I'm sensing that we need a break. A new activity and a fresh venue.

Theater Games: Holden in Dialogue

Next week I take the class down to the theater, which I've reserved for several days. Any larger, less desk-filled space than the classroom would do, but a stage helps suggest the nature of dialogue, how actual speech and gesture dramatize characters, make them "real," take them off the page. The students need to "hear" and "see" how Holden engages in dialogue and how he describes people's voices and gestures so that they'll be able to do this in their Holden's Voice piece. I divide them into groups of three or four. I warm them up, physically and vocally: jumping jacks with different sizes and speeds of jump; stretches and shake-outs. Nick, Julia, and Hunt, who take theater class, help us make various kinds of facial expressions and noises. Then I allot each group a scene from the book, roughly three pages with dialogue and narrative (with some duplication because it's interesting to see how different groups handle the same episode). I choose the scene on the train between Holden and a classmate's mother, Mrs. Morrow (70–73); the one in the cab in which Holden discusses with Horwitz, the driver, where the Central Park ducks go in winter (106–9); and two parts of Holden's discussion with Sally Hayes about running away together to live the simple life in Vermont (168–71 and 171–74).

The groups rehearse briefly and then perform their scenes, so that we all can get a clearer idea of how Salinger has Holden bring these memories to life for us, how dramatically the dialogue, the action, and Holden's thoughts are put together. I remind students that they'll be combining these three things when they write in Holden's voice: "If this were a play, of course his thoughts would have to be conveyed or implied *through* the dialogue and monologue. But it's a novel; there's a narrator. So I want each group to choose one person to play Holden as thinker and another as narrator."

I ask students to practice getting their heads out of their books whenever possible and using their eyes, their tone of voice, and some gestures to make the scene look and sound like a *real conversation.* They also need to figure out how to use their bodies and voices to convey the *location* of the scene to us—via movement and/or sounds. And finally, one more direction: they must try the first read-through with the person playing Holden's thoughts positioned at a *lower* level than the Holden who's speaking the dialogue, as well as *behind* him. This will help them keep track of the two Holdens, and it may create some other effects as well.

I circulate. "Don't be afraid to misread something. This is rehearsal. It's more important to get off the page and into your character. Who are you saying that line to? Can you look at her—even if you slow down and misread? Try it!" I stop all the groups, grab Nick and Julia, and we model half a page of reading with eye contact and movement, complete with stumbles. The kids see that it's okay to mess up a line, to lose your place, and that the scene's a lot more real with eye contact. Once they deliver a line actually looking at their partner, both actors' voices take on more expression. It's more fun this way, but for some students it's harder than annotating ten pages of text.

The taxicab groups get into the spirit quickly. In one of them, two kids stretch out on the floor horizontally as seats, one behind the other, making engine and brake noises, shaking back and forth over rough pavement, screeching to a halt at red lights. Horwitz is up front, driving, but turning his head to argue with Holden. Holden-as-narrator sits farthest back. Pretty soon, one of the train ride groups (Mrs. Morrow and Holden) begins to whistle at crossings, and the mother opens an imaginary magazine, adjusts her makeup, removes her gloves.

As groups enact their scenes, we all make discoveries: Holden's funny! He thinks his classmate Ernie is "about as sensitive as a goddam toilet seat" (72). And that's funnier because Ernie's mom has just said, "He's a very sensitive boy. He's really never been a terribly good mixer" (72). And how fast Holden can make up stories! (Whether it's lies or just imagining stuff.) Like telling Mrs. Morrow that Ernie refused out of modesty to be nominated for class president. And it's *funny,* worrying about the ducks when he's in a cab with this grumpy driver, and then how Horwitz gets really into the question, which you don't expect, and he's got a theory about "Mother Nature." You don't expect this tough, grumpy guy to say "Mother Nature."

"That's great! So when you become Holden and write about, say, Community Service Day, there'll probably be some funny moments, right? Listen, as we go on reviewing chapters this week, try to take the scenes off the page; "see" them and "hear" them. One more question: how did you figure out, as actors, what to *do*—I mean, with your bodies and your voice?"

"Well, the book often tells you. I hadn't noticed that," Ayana says. "My character, Mrs. Morrow, smiles a lot—she has a "nice" smile, she looks at her broken nail when she takes off her glove, she looks nice smoking because she doesn't 'wolf the smoke down like most older women.'"

"Yes, Holden—and, of course, Salinger—really helps you imagine the character. Even if you were just reading it to yourself, you could have a picture of her in your mind. So what might you conclude about Holden, if he gives you all this detail?"

"He notices a lot. I think he's really interested in people and has theories about them. But he generalizes a lot," says Julia. "Mothers do this, girls are always like that."

"Umm. With Holden it's *always* and *never,* isn't it. Do you think he's right that mothers will always believe anything wonderful you tell them about their sons, no matter how unlikely, and no matter how smart the mothers are? Well, save that one, because we're running out of time. Tonight I'll post these observations you've all made, so you'll have them to refer to when you become Holden."

The cab scenes both go very well. Garret makes a great cab driver. Jordan emerges from his silence to become Mrs. Morrow—his own choice. Students laugh, and when the two groups finish, Connor says, "I just noticed how in these scenes there's not much plain back-and-forth dialogue like in some books. I mean, not like in Hemingway. When someone says something, Holden tells you what he's noticed about the person or how he feels about what the guy just said. Mostly it's that way. I guess the very beginning of our scene has straight dialogue, but not much."

"Yes," Peter says, "you're hearing everything *through* Holden. He doesn't often get to have a long discussion with anyone. He notices lots of little details about them, which are really cool to read, because they don't just show you that person, they show you Holden, too. But what he keeps wanting—to have a real discussion with somebody—never happens. It's kind of sad."

Anna Quindlen on the Significant Detail

Peter's appreciation of Holden's reporting on details—and what these show us—leads me to Anna Quindlen's article in the *New York Times'* series, Writers on Writing: "The Eye of the Reporter, the Heart of the Novelist." Quindlen begins, "There's always a notebook in my purse." To capture the revealing detail. She tells us that as a reporter, the telling details—"the Yankees cap, the neon sign in the club window, the striped towel on the deserted beach"—when "taken incrementally, make a convincing picture of real life, and maybe get you onto Page 1, too." And, as a novelist, she says that the telling details "are the essence of fiction that feels real." They may be inventions—"the story, the people, the neighborhoods: they're all in my own mind"—now that she's become a novelist, but "the notebook still helps to keep the details fresh and true, to hold the quotations clear as consonants." This article should have appeal for my would-be newspapermen, James and Connor, and my readers and writers of sports reporting and athlete bios, Brooks, Matt, Garret, and Sarah, but also for my numerous devotees of suspense, horror, sci-fi, or romance. It has bearing on whatever type of writing they choose to try for their free-choice project, but more immediately, it's applicable to their piece in Holden's voice, which will combine reporting what actually happened to them with inventing Holden's experience of it.

Moreover, as relates to our work with dialogue in the theater games, Quindlen shows how a reporter's training is valuable in cultivating not just an eye for detail but also an *ear*: "I learned, from decades of writing down their words verbatim in notebooks, how real people talk. I learned that syntax and rhythm were almost as individual as a fingerprint, and that one quotation, precisely transcribed and intentionally untidied, could delineate a character in a way that pages of exposition never could." My writers need to hear this. And in light of their note-taking at our three grade 9 events, it doesn't hurt, either, that Quindlen makes a good case for carrying around a notebook.

To focus students on Salinger's use of detail in creating Holden's voice, I ask the class, "Remind me again, which ones of you have a strong preference for nonfiction over fiction? And the opposite? Okay, now because your next piece will partake of *both*, let's think for a moment about the differences—and the similarities, if you think there are some—between fiction and nonfiction. Let's start this thinking in your notebook." After five minutes of list-making, one of the similarities that emerges is *description*. And therefore, *details*. Then Peter suggests that both nonfiction and fiction can use *dialogue*. He mentions how we used quotes from our partners when we wrote the profile. "And besides dialogue, there's hearing a person's thoughts," he adds, perhaps remembering our game of Holden's Head. "You do that in novels, but you could also do it in a profile."

"Okay, descriptions and dialogue. Great. You all seem to agree that *description* needs details. What about dialogue? If you were trying to describe how Holden talks and thinks, what details might you include?"

"Oh, like the way he uses *phony* all the time," says Brooks. "And he ends a lot of sentences with 'and all.'"

"Good. And what about in nonfiction? Suppose you were describing the way some real person you know talks? Or if someone else were describing how you yourself talk?"

"Well, Ms. Michaels, how about you?" Nick shoots back.

"Fair enough, Nick. I know one detail right off—I use the verb *explore* all the time, when I'm talking about writing or reading or discussing. And I think Holden would probably notice that detail about me. He might like it—because it implies there's no single, right answer that I'm expecting students to find, and he likes that kind of freedom as opposed to how the speech teacher made them all shout 'Digression' whenever a student didn't stick to the topic. Or on the other hand, Holden might think it shows my phoniness. He might think that I just say it to make it *look* as if I'm really open-minded to whatever a student wants to find—and all."

The students seem interested now, so I hand out the Quindlen article and tell them that in this piece she's doing what we just did, explaining how both reporters and novelists look for details to use. I read aloud the opening paragraph and ask them to read the rest of the two pages silently, marking or annotating any points that interest them or that they think might be applicable to our work with Holden and Salinger. Circling the room, I'm pleased to see some people marking the passage: "I learned to distinguish between those details that simply existed and those that revealed." When everyone's finished, we begin to talk about some of Salinger's "revelatory details"—the red hunting hat that Holden wears backwards; Jane keeping all her kings in the back row in checkers; Phoebe continually inventing new middle names for herself. For homework I have them do the activities listed in Figure 3.2.

Next day, listening to the students' discussion of Holden's "sort of" and "really," I decide to give a quick lesson on *qualifiers* (sort of, kind of, in a way, by any chance, do you happen to know) and *intensifiers* (very, real, really, you really would, I really mean it, I'm not kidding). We talk about how much Holden/Salinger uses both kinds of expressions.

"Maybe it shows how anxious Holden is," Julia suggests. "Or, I know—it's because he cares so much about stuff, he can't just say it, he tries extra hard to say how *much* it matters, because a lot of people in the book just don't get it. And maybe he's afraid we won't get it either. So he'll say 'I really mean it.' I know I do that a lot when I'm talking to somebody."

---

1. Make **two** lists: one of details—specific words and expressions— that you feel help **characterize Holden's speech** and a second of details he observes or "digresses" to, that help **characterize his values, interests, views on life and people.**

2. Choose four or five items from your **first** list that you feel are especially "revelatory" or "telling" and write down **what you think they reveal.** Doing that will help you more, in the long run, with "becoming" Holden than just plugging in specific expressions and topics from your list. (Remember: I showed you an example of this process by analyzing my own use of *explore*: not just that it's a specific verb I use a lot but also what it might **reveal** about me. I offered you several ways it might characterize me—a positive one, from Holden's view anyway, and a negative one. You may find you need to do that with some of your four or five explanations, too.)

3. Do all this work **in your notebook**. I'll come around to check during free reading time tomorrow, and then we'll share findings— maybe in small groups. Would that work? That way you'd get to add to your own lists but you'd also have a chance to discuss what some of the expressions reveal.

FIGURE 3.2. STRATEGIES FOR BECOMING HOLDEN.

"Yeah. Or he'll swear—'helluva,' or 'so goddam much' or 'so damn depressed.' I guess that's the same sort of thing," Garret says.

"Yeah," says Connor. "And how about the other thing, the qualifiers? You tell us all the time not to use them when we're writing."

"Right—because they make you sound so cautious, as if you're not sure of yourself. The 'rather,' the 'somewhat,' the 'kind of': they drain off energy. But we use them a lot when we talk, as Julia said. So when you write in Holden's *speech* patterns, you can use anything that sounds like the way he talks. I think some of the qualifiers are also part of the Upper East Side speech patterns that he—and Salinger—would have grown up with, phrases considered genteel, refined—like when he asks a cab driver, 'Do you happen to know . . . by any chance . . .?'"

"He uses *you* pretty often," says Jenna. "Sometimes it's just the way you do when you mean 'everyone,' but other times it's like he's talking to us, personally. That kind of fits with what Julia said, about how he wants us to *get* what he's feeling. Like how he says 'you'd have really liked Allie.'"

The class has collected a lot of what Connor called "attitude words": *phony, lousy, crappy, nice, corny, swell, terrible, got a big bang out of, screwed-up, blue, depressed, terrific, get sore, madman, moron, stupid, boring, touchy, corny, pain in the ass, dopey, crazy, it kills me, it knocks you out, dopey, putrid, vomity-looking, I don't even like to talk about it, snobby, gave her the old eye, makes you want to puke.* But it's harder to talk about the rhythms and structure of Holden's sentences. So I decide we'll do something that I tried myself the night before as I wondered how today's discussion would go: copying a passage out by hand. I do this a lot with poems, sometimes just to slow myself down and listen better, sometimes because I want to memorize certain lines; but I rarely do it with prose. I chose a paragraph from Chapter 16, in which Holden visits the Museum of Natural History, and I wrote it out, keeping the same margins as our edition of *Catcher* has and using unlined paper—less distracting.

I took my old hunting hat out of my pocket while I walked, and put it on. I knew I wouldn't meet anybody that knew me, and it was pretty damp out. I kept walking and walking, and I kept thinking about old Phoebe going to that museum on Saturdays the way I used to. I thought how she'd see the same stuff I used to see, and how she'd be different every time she saw it. It didn't exactly depress me to think about it, but it didn't make me feel gay as hell either. Certain things they should stay the way they are. You ought

> to be able to stick them in one of those big glass cases and just leave them
> alone. I know that's impossible, but it's too bad anyway. Anyway, I kept
> thinking about all that while I walked. (158)

I found myself listening to the words and punctuation as they formed in my mind and took shape on my page. I could feel their length or shortness, their quickness or slowness; I was taking Holden's speech into my own breath. Writing by hand gave me time to feel him take his hunting hat out of his pocket and put it on, time to register the damp air, to hear the repetition of *ing* verbs, the walking and thinking, how his physical movement seemed to galvanize the working of memory—as it often does for me, when I go running and a combination of memory and rhythm starts a new poem writing itself inside my head.

What else did I notice, as I copied down this passage? How many of the sentences begin with *I*. How often the connector is *and*. How all the *ing* verbs help preserve the sensation of walking and thinking, of time passing, of unavoidable change. How by mid-paragraph, Holden moves into present tense, a much shorter sentence, and awkward, colloquial syntax with a double subject: "Certain things they should stay the way they are." This feeling goes deep for him. The museum glass cases, established as a literal image in earlier paragraphs, here become metaphor; it seems to help Holden clarify and crystallize his feelings about change, about growing up, even dying. The next sentence, with its two contradictory feelings connected with *but*, embodies his mix of acceptance and resistance: "I know that's impossible, but it's too bad anyway." And the final sentence returns us to the thinking and walking.

I could probably have arrived at this analysis intellectually by reading the passage a few times. But getting the sentences into my muscles and breath, watching and feeling my hand shaping them line by line, has allowed me to enter Holden more fully, body and mind, and appreciate how thoroughly Salinger did so.

I ask the students to find a paragraph of about half a page, one they particularly like, and copy it down by hand in their notebooks. "Yes, right now—not for homework. Don't rush. Do listen to the words and punctuation marks as you write them. Watch each sentence appearing on the page as your hand moves. I tried doing this last night and it was pretty interesting." I circle the room, curious to see each kid's choice. When they finish, I ask them to write down some things they noticed, felt, thought as they copied the passage. To reflect. Then we share our reflections. The consensus is that typing it on a laptop would be different—noisier, more distracting, faster. Somebody says copying by hand made her get quiet inside and hear Holden thinking, more than if she had just read the passage at home, where she'd be listening to her iPod. Someone else notices that his passage was similar to the dialogue from the scene he'd been in the other day: a few lines of back-and-forth arguing and then a lot of thoughts from Holden—how he felt and the things he noticed about the other person.

"I'm going to try this with some other parts of the book," Ayana says. "I think it would help me with sounding like Holden. In my paragraph, he started with these long sentences describing what's going on, and then they got shorter and shorter when he talked about how he breaks rules all the time to drive Stradlater crazy. And I also noticed that he uses *and* a lot to connect stuff in the longer sentences. I guess because that's the way we really talk when we're telling somebody about something that's happened."

"I noticed the *and* a lot in my passage too, Ayana. Salinger's been called a ventriloquist, because he made Holden's talking and thinking sound so real. If some of you didn't notice or 'hear' sentence lengths, you might try reading your passage aloud. That should help you. Ayana, could you read yours aloud to us?"

She does, and then I have her reread the last four sentences: "Besides, I did it to annoy Stradlater. It drove him crazy when you broke any rules. He never smoked in the dorm. It was only me" (54).

Connor's looking interested. "I think the earlier sentences are longer because they're all about this long silence going on between Holden and Stradlater after Holden gets mad and tears up the essay. These sentences kind of flow along with the *and*'s, like Ayana says. Then when Holden tells about how he breaks rules on purpose to annoy Stradlater, he talks in these short, jerky, nervous sentences, like jabbing at somebody. And also he's nervous about what could have happened with Jane on her date with Stradlater. That's another reason maybe for the short sentences. They sound tense."

"Do you all see how Salinger's rhythms get Connor into Holden's head? How the sentence lengths seem shaped by Holden's feelings—they seem natural, real—because Salinger's imagination has let him 'become' Holden. You can feel the nervous tension and you can see Holden, lying on the bed, smoking a cigarette, breaking the rules, and waiting for Stradlater to say something about the date with Jane. Fearing what he might say. When you begin writing your piece as Holden, listen to the voice you're creating—the individual words but also the sentence rhythms. As you read it aloud, be aware that sentence lengths and connectors can help you reflect his mood."

Your Life, Holden's, and Salinger's

In two more days we finish rereading the book. Our list of discussion questions continues to grow on the wall, and certain students' quickwrites are finally getting longer and richer. I take part of a class period for one more quickwrite: on "your own present feelings about being a kid versus growing up." It seems to help clarify, or complicate, their view of Holden. Ambivalence is easier to understand in relation to one's own feelings than to those of a fictional character, or even those of a friend. Also, perhaps we're more indulgent of our own inconsistencies. Less quick to label them "hypocrisy." Most of the students agree that sometimes they want to be older and to have people treat them as "mature," but other times they really dread leaving home, finding work, getting "tied down" or "stuck in something boring"— and, as one writes, "being like my parents." Some still go trick-or-treating, have snowball fights, bring water pistols to school, throw food. "Sometimes you just need to be silly. We're still kids," Nick says, "and there's too much pressure about grades and college and stuff."

I steal one more day in order to show clips from a film about Salinger that I first saw at a National Council of Teachers of English Annual Convention. As writers, the students need, I think, to consider the way personal experience and imagination can weave together to create a work of art—to reveal emotional truth. I ask the students to take notes as we watch the clips—"on anything that interests you, of course, but particularly on aspects of Salinger's life or character that you could imagine contributing to his creation of Holden and Holden's journey. We can't know whether our imaginings are correct—but you may find it interesting to speculate. Your piece in Holden's voice is going to combine *your own experience* of whichever event you choose to retell *and your imagining* of how Holden might live that experience."

The class seems eager to make connections. What interests them the most, especially some of the boys, is Salinger's war experience: landing at

Utah Beach; being engaged in the Battle of the Bulge; his subsequent hospi-talization for "battle fatigue"; and, after his recovery, staying on in Europe past the end of the war, tracking down Nazis.

"So does *battle fatigue* mean post-traumatic stress disorder?" asks Peter. "Maybe that's where he got the idea for D.B.'s reaction to the army and the war."

"And maybe," says Jess quietly, "that helped him imagine Holden's depression and thoughts of suicide. Maybe that's why Holden's always say-ing that he's nervous, and he feels like he might disappear. And sometimes that he wants to die. Could you maybe say those feelings are, like, his 'dark descent'—like to the Underworld?"

"Yeah," Jenna agrees. "Maybe Salinger was kind of obsessed with see-ing guys killed and depressing things like that and he wanted to create this really obsessed person who's, like, falling apart and keeps obsessing about phonies. And has this dead brother he talks to."

"So it's worth thinking about how writing—your own, as well as the books you read—may grow partly, consciously or subconsciously, from aspects of the writer's experience, but *transformed by imagination*. You may become aware of this happening as you write your next piece."

Writing Holden's Narrative—Ways to Start

We need to start writing this piece. I ask students to review the notes they made at the three events they attended, decide which one they're going to use, review their lists of "Holden details," and then start drafting "his" account of this event—at least one full typed page. I'm not asking them to suggest goals or criteria for assessment yet, because they'll have a clearer idea of what's possible and what's problematic once they've started to write. I just ask them to keep in mind, as they work, our various observa-tions of how Holden talks and thinks and how Salinger constructs scenes or episodes. "Think back over whatever you remember best from these past three weeks—all your questions that are up on the wall, our quickwrites, discussions, theater games, Quindlen's article, copying passages, and read-ing aloud. They can all help you." And I ask them to send me by class time tomorrow—preferably tonight—a copy of what they've written.

"But Ms. Michaels, how should we start?" Garret asks, sounding worried.

"Put up your hands, anyone else who has the same question." A lot of hands. "So thanks, Garret. Notice, you're not alone. But I think you all can come up with some possibilities."

"Maybe look at how Salinger starts chapters," suggests Hunt. "I think sometimes they start with Holden just saying some idea he's got on his mind, or maybe where he's going next and, like, what time of day it is."

"Yes, and remember that you can refer to other things Holden's just done or is thinking about or remembering before this particular experience. That could come from the book, or you could make up something that's in keeping with his story and character."

"There's a lot about going places—trains, walking, cabs. So you could start with that—how he gets to the whatever-it-is and what happens on the way there," says Connor.

"Or he could be thinking about what's about to happen—and connecting it to similar things he's been through, and making predictions and talking to us—like 'You'd think missing a day of school would be really swell, but . . . ,' and then he'd generalize about how these things always turn out to be so phony," Julia says, laughing. "I think we should get into his attitude right off."

Garret's hand is up, waving. "Hey, maybe he's, like, a new kid, like his parents sent him here after he flunks out somewhere else, so he's checking everybody out, comparing us to his other schools."

"Okay, great. See, I didn't have to say a word. You folks are full of ideas. Maybe we can brainstorm in pairs tomorrow if you each get a good start on your own tonight. Some people may want to jot down ideas first and then write; I tend to be the messy kind of thinker who just plunges in and keeps crossing out stuff as I go. Whatever works for you."

Troubleshooting and Setting Criteria

Next day, while everyone does free reading, I skim any draft openings that I didn't get to check ahead of time. Good starts, mostly, though a few have gotten hung up on tedious descriptions of the school buses, and quite a few have peppered their page with swear words and *phonies* in their effort to be Holden. Garret's obviously having a good time with his piece:

It was a brisk September day when I was walking around school after fenc-
ing and I bumped into one of the biggest phonies you will ever meet. Garret Cummings. He was strutting around with his chin up and all and his
hair slicked back like a real hot shot. I think he really is a lousy sonuvabitch.
He really is. He said, "Holden, you going to the Homecoming cookout?"
I said, "What? Oh you mean the thing with the skits and hamburgers." It
took him a second to process because he was so thick headed but then he
mumbled, "Yeah, that one."

Later, when we work with partners and James is reading Garret's aloud,
he stops to ask what makes Holden call the guy a "lousy sonuvabitch." I'd
wanted to ask the same question.

James says, "I can see he thinks he's a hot shot because of the way he
struts and slicks his hair, and he comes off as pretty stupid, but so far he
doesn't do anything really *lousy*."

"Yeah, but Holden says it a lot," Garret protests. "Lousy sonuvabitch."

"But more for somebody who's done something really bad, like Maurice.
Maybe you could use it later, for something worse." Garret nods and crosses
it out. A little farther down the page, James pauses again. "You want me to
say wherever it stops sounding like Holden, right? Well, here he says 'That
really sucks.' That sounds more like you." Garret grins and crosses it out.

I call all the kids back into the circle and ask what problems have been
coming up, or what they think might be hard to do as they finish telling the
story.

"I think I'm taking too long to get into what actually happens," Jess worries. "I have him reacting to all these kids on the bus and thinking about
his last school, and feeling lonely and wishing Allie were with him. I mean,
Salinger's chapters are at least six or seven pages. How long are these supposed to be?"

"Well, let's get a list on the board of what you think you need to include.
Whether you chose Community Service Day or the peer group retreat or the
Homecoming weekend, you've got some basic action he'd talk about, right?
But he doesn't have to describe everything that happened and every person
he talks to or reacts to. How will you choose?"

There's a long silence. This is hard. Finally Peter says, "Well, I'd choose
the things I can guess Holden would have strong reactions to. And ones

where he might make connections, or digressions, that show something about him, about what he's like."

"That sounds good, Peter. Could you give an example?"

"Maybe, for the Community Service Day—that's what I'm doing—I'd have him tell about when we were given shears and rakes and gloves and the guy explained which plants were the invasive species and needed to be cut. In my notes, I had Holden reacting to the idea of invasive species—that they have just as much a right to be there, and how anyway none of the guys were listening to the ranger, 'cause he did look sort of weird, all scrawny in these big boots and waving little sprigs around at us, and so they just started whacking away at anything green. And I think Holden's going to get depressed and sneak off into the woods to the lake, and maybe . . . I don't know. I guess he'll have a dialogue with somebody—maybe there's this kid playing by the lake, or some girl. . . ."

"I'm doing the peer retreat," Hunt says, "and I think I want to have him tell about the skits because he has all these thoughts about acting and what's phony about it. But I don't know how to get a dialogue in there. I don't think there's room to describe all the different games we played."

"I want to have him tell about those dumb games where we had to answer questions—he'd probably just make up stuff and maybe think about what a terrific liar he is. And the game where we had to partner up and learn two new things about the person. That could be dialogue, I guess," Brooks offers.

I've been writing on the board as they talk:

> narrow down to one or two activities that Holden would react strongly to
> activities that could produce dialogue
> activities that trigger memories? digressions?

And I add:

> choose the *revelatory* details—streamline the descriptions.

"So what sort of criteria should we set up for you to use in drafting the rest, for peer response, and for final assessment? For the next few minutes, why don't you each make a list on the laptops of things you think are important both to make the piece sound like Holden's voice and mind and to make it a strong, interesting story. Send it to me, and I'll combine them and post a list tonight so you'll have it as you go on writing. Shall we shoot for three typed pages for the total piece? Think you can make that fit? With a complete draft for peer response the day after tomorrow? We could work on it in class tomorrow, too. And if you have questions tonight, email me. Or make an appointment at the Writing Center." A few groans at the deadline but no downright rebellion.

That night I post their criteria. It's interesting that although we haven't recently mentioned "strong conclusion," students seem to have internalized this from their work on our previous pieces, along with "good opening hook" and "catchy title." But in addition, we have "sounds like Holden—his words, expressions, sentences," "shows his attitudes." Some students list *specific* attitudes: "mix of humor and depression, mood shifts," "obsession with phonies," "looking for intelligent discussions, loneliness," "concern with unfairness, inequality," "cynicism, loss of innocence," "wanting to protect children/childhood," "fear of being yellow," "fear of growing up/trying to grow up" "confusion about sex/girls," "frustration with school." Then we have "dialogue mixed with H's thoughts," "good choice of events that reflect his attitudes," "good balance of action and thinking," "significant details—to reveal Holden," and "combines real experience with inventing." I post *all* of these items so students can see what they and their peers produced and can refer to the list as they write. The list may help keep the more reductive thinkers and readers from presenting too simplistic a picture of Holden. But for assessment purposes, I boil down their ideas and add a couple of my own (see Figure 3.3).

For the peer response sheet, which should reflect these four criteria but break them down into more specific skills-related questions that will elicit practical help from each student's partner, I try to curb my enthusiasm for covering all possible bases. I remind myself of the ADHD students, of the restiveness of fourteen-year-olds. I include at the top of the page, as a reminder, (1) the list of Holden's values or attitudes that I collected from their emails. I include (2) my four assessment criteria, also as a reminder. Next, (3) the directions, then (4) room for the writer's specific requests, then (5) some questions, and finally, (6) some space at the end for the responder to write an overall comment about the draft.

In phrasing the various items, I've tried to ensure that the authors get some specific praise—for effective creation of voice, use of details, revelation of character—not the generalized "awesome piece" or "nice job." And in

I will assess and grade your piece on the basis of:

1. How well it reflects your understanding of Salinger's presentation of Holden—his character, his voice, and his journey

2. How convincingly you use Holden's language (words, expressions, sentence rhythms) and his habit of detailed observation to retell your experience imaginatively from his point of view

3. How effectively and thoughtfully you combine narrative, dialogue, and reflection within the three-page limit

4. How well you use your opportunities for developing the piece—via your annotations and preliminary notes, discussions of drafting, peer responses, conferences, and revising and editing

FIGURE 3.3. *Assessment criteria.*

item 6, I'm hoping for insight into the responder's reading ability, her understanding of Holden's character as reflected (or not) in her partner's draft, and also into her ability to write analytically and critically in full sentences, not just to annotate.

Everyone will have two days for revising after peer response, during which time they may sign up for a conference with a writing mentor if they choose. We spend the entire period on the peer response. I try to visit each pair, initially to check on the specificity of authors' requests and to watch the lipreading, later to make sure authors' requests have been addressed. Near the end of the period, I ask everyone to write on the back of their own draft at least one or two things they plan to work on during the next two days of revision. We go around the circle to share these plans and reinforce the idea that *everyone* has had second thoughts.

Two days later, when the revisions come in, I ask everyone to write, on the back of the revised draft, a couple of things they like about the piece and a couple of changes they'd make if they had more time. This information nearly always helps me decide how to start a conference on the piece and how to focus my written comments. This time, with the future free-choice project in mind, I also ask students to make some notes on what they think they learned from writing the piece. And finally, since we've spent nearly a month with *Catcher*, I ask them for a couple of sentences about what stands out for them in their experience of reading and rereading the book.

Two Partners' Work

That night, as I look over the revised drafts, I'm struck by how much this assignment asks of these students and how much imagination they've brought to it. Perhaps the greatest challenge for some was moving beyond their initial view of Holden as a chronic and unjustified complainer. Then the next struggle was to capture convincingly within the confines of three pages the way his mind moves. A few students threw in the towel after two pages. Jordan, who had no notes from his peer retreat day, crammed his material into one and a half pages, totally free of dialogue and perpetrating such high-speed, information-packed sequences as: "I wish everybody were good to me that way, like Phoebe. Sometimes my parents just don't seem to care enough. I guess it's because I'm growing up and all, now I have to go on my own. Soon it will be smooth sailing to living out west as a deaf-mute." In the margins of the rough draft, Brooks had written to him, tactfully: "Maybe digress longer on Phoebe?" and "You show how Holden doesn't find many things fun, but you might want to find something/someone he likes/enjoys? Might add some dialogue." While Jordan took a couple of simpler suggestions—moving two related sentences closer together, for example—he didn't tackle the more demanding ones.

I remind myself that this is a student who in his previous school had written very little apart from timed "take a stand" prompts, and for whom "global revision" may be a pretty new concept. On a separate sheet, I write suggestions—reinforcing Brooks's—for an optional extra revision, but first I praise Jordan's recognition of some important feelings of Holden's about his family and his future. I make a note to myself to work on comma splices in a small-group conference that will include Jordan. I pencil into my grade book a ghost grade—a grade that can change if the writer revises the revision successfully or if, in conference, we find strengths I hadn't seen on my first reading. I'll ask Jordan to read the piece aloud to me and tell me some things he likes about it and what he might do if he had more time, since he didn't list any positives or negatives before he turned it in. Then we'll go over the four criteria for assessment to see how he'd rate the piece on each of them and arrive at a grade. I'll explain ghost grades, but as I know he's having a tough time in most of his courses, I won't be surprised if he chooses not to revise the piece any further. He's already learned a lot—assumed a persona, moved from narrative to reflection and back again, taken and given criticism in the peer response. His suggestions to Brooks include "make sure the slang is for Holden's generation and not now; work on a better ending, don't just stop; sometimes too many Holdenisms." His paragraph on how Brooks reflects Holden's values and feelings is too brief, but at least it offers one specific point (though reflecting a superficial reading of Holden's character): "You had the overall idea of how Holden was throughout *Catcher in the Rye*. In the story you showed how Holden had his mind focused on something that no one else would, like when Holden was curious where the ducks go in the winter."

Brooks, on the other hand, has turned in a surprisingly fat packet: the initial notes, the draft for peer response, a second draft with a new digression about Phoebe, and a third draft with a new ending. He's removed the anachronistic slang, cut back on the Holdenisms so they don't fall into awkward clumps, and clarified the setting at the outset of the piece. Comma splices, lack of pagination, and some errors in punctuating dialogue are items he could have fixed; Jordan had warned him about the comma splices, in fact. But I pencil a tentative A- into my grade book and wait to see how he will assess the piece when we apply the criteria in conference. We'll go over his feedback on Jordan's piece, also.

So Far/What Next?

Skimming everyone's notes on what they learned from writing this story, I'm feeling that the class is already better prepared for the free-choice piece than my last year's students were. Certainly they're in better shape to write a story. Using the full day of activities they'd actually experienced—peer retreat or Community Service Day or Homecoming games—helped free them to think about ways to structure a narrative since they didn't have to invent an entire plot. The necessity of telling about the day from Holden's point of view was also freeing, though it created some challenges. They discovered that describing events in chronological order, including every detail and sticking strictly to factual truth, wouldn't necessarily serve to reveal the narrator's character convincingly. They had to think creatively. Moreover, writing in a voice other than their own made many of them listen more carefully to word choice and sentence rhythms. For the first time, at least this year, they were combining narrative, reflection, and dialogue; I think they are becoming aware of the different possibilities that each of these three mediums offers the storyteller. For some, this is the longest piece they've ever written, and certainly the most complex. And, finally, they've had the opportunity to see how fiction and nonfiction, or invention and fact, can operate together within a work of art.

Now that they've experienced reading *Catcher* as writers, motivated by the need to use Salinger's techniques and the voice he created for Holden in a story of their own, students should be in a better position to write a short piece of literary analysis—to argue the case for their own interpretation of a literary work.

As we respond together to the next journey, Athol Fugard's play *"Master Harold" . . . and the boys* (set in South Africa shortly before apartheid became law), I'll try to stay focused on what this work can teach us about writing. We'll read in the playwright's journal an incident from his teenage years that lies at the emotional core of *"Master Harold"* and then watch, as the play unfolds, how he transforms this private moment into a public drama in which the personal is also the political. Fugard's unresolved ending invites individual interpretation and offers opportunities for self-reflection as well as analysis and argument. I think this complex of responses can offer my students new and useful writing challenges that will open up additional possibilities for their free-choice project.

Other Stories Told by Young Narrators Whose Voices a High School Writer Might Adopt

There are many good first-person narratives in high school English curricula, but this writing assignment works best with a young and fairly contemporary narrator who has a lively, well-defined voice and some "attitude."

Alvarez, Julia. *In the Time of the Butterflies*
Cisneros, Sandra. *The House on Mango Street*

Frank, Anne. *The Diary of a Young Girl*
Lee, Harper. *To Kill a Mockingbird*
Paterson, Katherine. *Bridge to Terabithia*
Twain, Mark [Clemens, Samuel]. *Adventures of Huckleberry Finn*
Wolff, Tobias. *This Boy's Life*

Chapter 4

Taking a Stand: Analysis, Argument, Persuasion

Sam Semele—Basuto—with the family fifteen years. Meeting him again when he visited Mom set off string of memories.

The kite which he produced for me one day during those early years when Mom ran the Jubilee Hotel and he was a waiter there. He had made it himself: brown paper, its ribs fashioned from thin strips of tomato-box plank which he had smoothed down, a paste of flour and water for glue. I was surprised and bewildered that he had made it for me.

I vaguely recall shyly "haunting" the servants' quarters in the well of the hotel—cold, cement-gray world—the pungent mystery of the dark little rooms—a world I didn't understand. Frightened to enter any of the rooms. Sam, broad-faced, broader based—he smelled of woodsmoke. The "kaffir smell" of South Africa is the smell of poverty—woodsmoke and sweat.

Later, when he worked for her at the Park café, Mom gave him the sack: ". . . he became careless. He came late for work. His work went to hell. He didn't seem to care no more." I was about thirteen and served behind the counter while he waited on table.

Realise now he was the most significant—the only—friend of my boyhood years. On terrible windy days when no-one came to swim or walk in the park, we would sit together and talk. Or I was reading—Introductions to Eastern Philosophy or Plato and Socrates—and when I had finished he would take the book back to New Brighton.

> Can't remember now what precipitated it, but one day there was a rare
> quarrel between Sam and myself. In a truculent silence we closed the café,
> Sam set off home to New Brighton on foot and I followed a few minutes lat-
> er on my bike. I saw him walking ahead of me and, coming out of a spasm
> of acute loneliness, as I rode up behind him I called his name, he turned in
> mid-stride to look back and, as I cycled past, I spat in his face. Don't sup-
> pose I will ever deal with the shame that overwhelmed me the second after
> I had done that (25–26).

From South African playwright Athol Fugard's Notebooks, *1960–1977*

Commentary

We're reading Athol Fugard's play, *"Master Harold". . . and the boys.* Since I
want to make each text and writing assignment this term contribute to the
free-choice writing project, I started by focusing on the *genesis* of Fugard's
play—how it grew out of his confronting a painful memory from his teenage years. I wanted us to read and hear the play as writers with memories
and biases of our own that we might explore and that might help us connect
with the racial tensions between Fugard's characters: two black men and a
white boy in 1950s South Africa. I wanted my writers to appreciate how a
full-length play can flower from the seed of a single memory, if that memory is tended by the writer's imagination. So here is where we began, with
the notebook entry that lies at the heart of the play, an entry written about
twenty years before the first production. I copied the two pages to hand out
along with the *Notebooks'* cover photo of Fugard, profile of a dark-bearded
white South African looking out at us over his shoulder.

　　I also copied the cover of our Penguin edition of the play—two black actors, Danny Glover and the South African Zakes Mokae, playing the waiters,
Willie and Sam, and Zeljko Ivanek as the teenage white boy, Hally (from
the 1982 Yale Repertory Theater production). In our rereading of *Catcher in
the Rye,* we had viewed photos of Salinger on video and considered possible
connections between his life and Holden's—between life and literature, fact
and fiction, between two different kinds of truth. Now here we had Fugard—
his photo and his notebook entry—and the actors playing characters in the
play based, in part, on his life.

Exploring a Memory

We start with some reflective quickwrites. I first read aloud the entry from *Notebooks*, slowly, asking the class to listen for and mark any words that help them *feel* the power that this memory of anger and shame has for Fugard—feel why he would choose to write it down. I ask them how they might categorize these words.

"Well," says Connor slowly, "there's all the descriptions—of the kite, the guys' rooms, the smell. It seems like when he's going back to those days, all his senses are coming alive."

"And some of the words are about feelings," says Sydney. "Like *surprised* and *bewildered, frightened, truculent, shame.*"

"And *spasm of acute loneliness*," adds Peter. "That's the most interesting one. You hate him when he tells how he spit at Sam, but it seems like you could feel a little sorry for him, too, because he's just maybe lost the only friend he has, and the spit is this pain coming out. It's the spasm, like he's doubled up with pain and sort of can't stop himself from letting it out."

"Yeah, but it's disgusting that he would do that!" Jess exclaims. "And, uh, I don't know how it was back then, whenever this happened, back in South Africa, but if all the whites called black grown-up men 'boy,' even if he liked these two guys he might think they had no right to argue with him. Like, he's above them. So he spits at Sam because he's mad Sam would dare to argue. He says it's a *rare* argument, so I guess he's not used to Sam doing that?"

"Do you think when he was writing this he was thinking about anyone reading it?" Julia wonders. "I mean, you said this entry becomes the center of the play, but at the time he was just freewriting like what we do, right? And it seems really private, not something he'd want to show anyone. But the writing's so detailed, like it's for readers. I think if I'd done that to a friend, I wouldn't want anybody to know. And I wouldn't even want to write about it."

"Anyone else wondering about this?" I ask. Several hands go up.

"Maybe even if he didn't know he'd write a play later on, he was just so ashamed that he had to kind of punish himself, force himself to remember all the details to, like, get rid of the guilt?" Jenna suggests. Several heads nod, and Garret mutters, "Wow, deep."

"It might be interesting to look at the introduction to *Notebooks* and see if it says anything about this," I offer, and open my copy. I read aloud:

> They [the *Notebooks*] became a habit, serving many purposes—at one level a constant literary exercise which I hoped would lead to greater accuracy in expression. Without them my thinking and feeling would be confused, blurred. I never quite understand the chemistry of my relationship with them. Sometimes it was compulsive, at others I wrote nothing. They reflect a certain reality in terms of the South African experience but although I have lived through very major political crises, these are not reflected. And though I never consciously used the notebooks as a playwright, everything is reflected there—my plays come from life and from encounters with actual people. But I found that as soon as I got deeply involved with writing a play, I either forgot the notebooks completely or had no need of them. (8)

"And here's another useful bit, where the editor of the *Notebooks*, Mary Benson, explains that Fugard used short extracts from them in introductions to his published plays, and then, later, was encouraged to consider publishing a wider selection, so he finally asked her to edit the original *Notebooks* for publication. So, Julia, what we're reading may not be *exactly* what he first wrote, though my guess is that the editing consisted mainly of cutting out passages here and there—not of polishing the writing. The reviewer from *Time* who's quoted on the back cover calls this 'raw diary form.'"

"So it's kind of both," Sydney says. "I mean, he goes into detail to make himself be accurate in his writing. It's not like he's thinking it will be published. And he does use the notes for his plays in a way, like subconsciously. The stuff stays in his mind maybe because he's writing in such detail. So he doesn't even *need* to look back at the notebook when he's writing the play."

"Yes, that sounds right. It's interesting that he says he himself isn't quite clear about how he relates to the notebooks. But he uses them to avoid blurry, confused thinking. And he's trying to get not just the facts accurate, but the *feelings*. So before we start reading the play, let's try *writing*. Think about a hard-to-face memory of your own—not to create a play, but to understand what Fugard's shame might feel like—and also, as a writer, to see how accurately you can remember a moment. I think doing this may help us connect to the characters later on, too, especially to Hally, who's only three years older than most of you. We can start right now, and then add more tonight, as we remember more.

> Close your eyes and think back to some event—something you did or said to somebody else, or maybe something you *didn't* do, some time you let something bad go on and didn't intervene—that you feel ashamed about. Maybe you immediately felt the shame or maybe it hit you later, I don't know. And perhaps it's something you feel you still haven't "dealt with," as Fugard says about the episode with Sam. Let's try to remember as many details as we can in order to "avoid blurry thinking." Try making your mind into a screen and see the moment coming into focus—colors, sounds, feelings. This is a private piece—I won't look at it, though I'll cruise around to make sure you've done it. Because tomorrow we'll talk about the process of remembering and writing, and what shame feels like and whether there are ways to get rid of it. And then I think we'll be ready to start reading the play. Keep your eyes closed a bit longer. See what starts coming back to you. . . .

The Nature of Shame

The next day several students note that this was a difficult assignment, not just because some of these moments go back a long time but because "it hurt to go there." They agree that Fugard was brave to write about what he did to Sam, though Nick, the pragmatist, thinks maybe it was easier for him "because he knew that he wanted to be a writer and describing this memory in his notebook would help him get better at writing."

I ask the class how, based on the memory they wrote about, they think shame registers in their bodies. And how might they try to cover it up—from others, even from themselves. What does it take to get rid of the sensation, to expunge the awareness of wrongdoing? And why do they still remember it? Some students talk of trying to rationalize it, or make excuses so they'll feel less guilty. Several say they tried to "make it up" to the person they'd hurt, while others admit they are still avoiding the person. "I couldn't face her," Sarah says, "but I've tried hard, ever since, to not say those things, especially when I'm with a group of kids who like to joke about it. But it's hard because then they start making fun of me. They act like I'm inferior or something."

"Somewhere recently I read a line that seems relevant here: that no one can make you believe you're inferior unless you let them," I say tentatively.

"Yeah," says Jordan. "That's something my mom says."

I notice that Sarah and Jordan, two of the students who participate the least in whole-class discussions about assigned reading and who tend to make the fewest annotations in their texts, are more comfortable and engaged when the talk turns to personal experience. I hope that grounding the play in personal memory may help make the reading register as "experience" for them, not just as homework.

"Maybe other people can't make you really believe you're inferior," says Nick, "but it hurts even if you just think that *they* believe it."

A lot of kids nod vigorously. "Do you think it's possible," I ask, as the period's about to end, "that Fugard's spitting at Sam after their argument could have been motivated not just by loneliness and, as Jess said yesterday, by his racist sense of superiority to Sam, but also by a feeling of *inferiority*? I don't think we can answer that yet about Hally in the play, but just in terms of human psychology, could a person feel both superior and inferior at the same time? For different reasons?" I write my own question up on the wall. It will keep.

Personal/Political: Will Sam and Hally Repair Their Friendship?

As we read the play, I keep pushing the students to *imagine it differently from what's on the page—to read as writers.* What would we lose if the phone calls from Hally's mother and his hospitalized father weren't there? Does Fugard gain anything by keeping the two parents off-stage? It's important for us, as readers and writers, to be able to imagine various possibilities for the text so that we can weigh Fugard's choices. Which details, for instance, has he kept or expanded from the original notebook entry? Jess notices how the kite-making reappears with a lot of new details—"It takes up, like, three pages, and I think that's gonna be important later on. Because Hally says he felt so proud when they got it to fly, and then he says it feels time for another kite." James points out how the discussions of philosophy, mentioned in the *Notebooks*, are turning out to be "really big" in the play—how Hally and Sam's discussion of what constitutes a "man of magnitude," and what famous men might qualify, is a long one with lots of arguing. "It shows their differences, but they end up finding one person they can agree on." I mention a later notebook entry on Sam teaching ballroom dancing, which will also become very important in later scenes. "So these items—the kite flying, the philosophy discussions, the ballroom dancing—were all givens, factually true, in that Fugard remembers them clearly as part of his personal experience with Sam; but as the playwright he has to decide whether and how to expand them and explore their meaning. And invent new things."

Over the next few days of reading, we watch the tension grow between Hally and Sam. Kids are starting to notice Hally's sense of superiority to Sam and to wonder how Sam can be so patient. They're uncomfortable with Hally's mixed feelings toward his crippled, alcoholic, racist father, about to come home from the hospital, and with Hally's refusal to acknowledge Sam's generous mentoring. They understand the spitting better when they see Fugard build the scene: Hally, driven by shame for his father and a need to assert status as a white male, using his father's racist joke against Sam and Sam's response. They start to recognize the poignancy of how the ballroom dancing that we saw Sam and Willy practicing together for a regional competition grows from a literal image into a metaphor for peace—peace within families but also between races and countries. As Sam explains to Hally: "To be one of those finalists on that dance floor is like . . . like being in a dream about a world in which accidents don't happen." There are no collisions out there.

> And it's beautiful because that is what we want life to be like. But instead, like you said, Hally, we're bumping into each other all the time. Look at the three of us this afternoon. . . . And it doesn't stop with us. The whole world is doing it all the time. Open a newspaper and what do you read? America has bumped into Russia, England is bumping into India, rich man bumps into poor man. Are we never going to get it right? . . . Learn to dance life like champions instead of always being just a bunch of beginners at it? (46)

This speech helps the class realize that Sam and Hally's struggling friendship invites us to explore both the personal and the political. When we debate and write about whether the ending makes us feel that their relationship will survive, we'll have to consider not just two personalities but also racial conflicts within an entire society. Watching excerpts of a video

of South Africa's Truth and Reconciliaton hearings helps the students understand something of life under apartheid—the legalized racism that was
just about to take hold when Hally and Sam were living out their complex
relationship.

I hold off discussion of the final reading assignment until each student
has gathered textual evidence to support two opposite interpretations of
the play's ending. We use these paragraphs in a spirited class debate and
then, somewhat grudgingly, the students revise their paragraphs, drawing
on some of the fresh evidence and ideas they gained from listening to both
teams. Revision is grudging because, I think, for them the debate was the
climax of this literature study. For ninth graders, argument is much more
fun face-to-face and out loud than on the page, where correct incorporating and citing of evidence, construction of subordinate clauses, and clear
transitions from one point to the next are an annoying imposition. And who
was their audience supposed to be? They'd already heard everyone's ideas,
after all. I could see that if the art of persuasive writing was to come alive
for them, they each needed to argue an issue of their own—a cause rooted
in personal experience and knowledge that they could share with the rest of
us.

"The Danger of Countenance": Taking a Stand in Writing, in Life

To kick off the final writing of this unit and offer a model, I give the students Tom Romano's *English Journal* article, "The Danger of Countenance,"
about an incident from his high school days when he "countenanced" racism. We start reading it aloud in class. Analyzing the impact of race on the
selection of the prom queen's escort, Romano condemns his own passive
acceptance of his town and school's status quo and his coach's decision.
The article can offer my students a helpful bridge between racism in South
Africa—which feels comfortably remote to many of them even if they do
come to care about Sam and Hally—and racism in our own communities.
Even though Romano describes a high school in the 1960s, that's still a
much more familiar setting and thus helps bring racism closer to home. I
hope these kids will find in Romano's story the inspiration to *reflect* on their
own ability to take a stand on a controversial issue. But with the free-choice
project in mind, I also want them to see how Romano is combining several

writing modes: narrating and reflecting on a personal experience to illus-trate an argument and make a point.

I remind students of the private quickwrite they did at the start of this unit in relation to Fugard's diary entry, re-creating a personal episode that made them feel ashamed, and I explain that Tom Romano has done some-what the same thing here, but with the additional purpose of illustrating an argument, one he's had with himself and one he's having with his readers. Before we start reading the piece aloud, I give them directions (see Figure 4.1) for tonight's homework. I take time to read a page of the article aloud and then stop. "So he's given us this story, this memory; it's the first page of a five-page piece. Let's consider two things: As a *writer*, do you see some directions you could go from here if *you* were developing the article? And as a *reader,* what questions do you have at this point? What would you like to know, to hear about, in the next few pages? Why don't you make two lists, quickly, one as writer and one as reader. Then as you read tonight, you can see whether Romano covers any of these things." The first activity overlaps with the second. They'll begin to realize this as the same items start to reap-pear on both of their lists. I want students to see the value of asking them-selves, as writers, "What else would *my reader* want to hear about?"

Next day we all write for five minutes or so on our feelings about the story and how we might have felt or acted in that situation. Then, because I think this may be a hard story to talk about initially in a large group, I break the students into threesomes to share whatever they've been writing. As I listen in, I notice that all the groups start with Romano's story and how it answered most of their questions; then they gradually move to their own experiences, especially of "countenancing" things by keeping quiet. Many of the white kids insist that multiracial friendships and dating are "no big prob-lem at our school" and mention a few specific couples, but some students of color disagree. Several say that often friendships don't go much beyond sports—team practices and games and parties. Others say there's a gender difference; that girls' parties are less likely to be multiracial than guys' are. Finally I ask, "So what do you think about Romano's idea that countenanc-ing something you don't agree with—staying silent about something you think is bad—is the same as sanctioning it, approving it, and makes you *complicit?*" A majority of them agree, though there's some lively argument. "So are there certain bad things you might *countenance* and others you'd stand up against?" I ask them.

1. Finish reading Romano's article about a guilty memory from his own high school past. **Mark** phrases that help put you into his situation and enter his feelings (both at the time of the event and as he looks back).

2. **Consider** how the author defines *systemic racism* and *countenance* and **copy down** the phrases that help you understand these terms.

3. Think over your own feelings about the episode and what you would have done if you'd been in Romano's place. And the coach's place. And Greg's, and Amy's. We'll be writing a little in class tomorrow about this, as a preliminary to discussion.

FIGURE 4.1. *PRELIMINARIES TO DISCUSSING ROMANO'S ARTICLE.*

"It's easier to take a risk if it's for a friend of yours," says Sydney. "I think if I'd been Greg, I'd be really mad that Tom didn't stand up for me, but Greg doesn't get mad."

"But there are some things where it wouldn't matter if it was a friend or not," says Jessica. "Where you just believe so strongly that you have to do something."

"Writing is a way to figure out what those particular things might be," I tell them. "See how Romano used it to ask himself *why he was complicit*, and how he considers a lot of possible answers? Now he could have just written this as a *private* reflection for himself. Did you see any signs in the writing that made you feel he was trying to reach you and keep you interested? That this was a *public* piece?

"I liked how he told several stories in it—the one about Homecoming, with Greg and Amy and the coach, and then some stories about his own growing up, with his family and the birthday party when he was little and those parents who wouldn't let their kids come if his mom invited his black friends but he said he wanted them so she did," says Connor all in one breath.

"And I like how he uses dialogue and quotes part of that Langston Hughes poem. Oh, and repetition. He makes that really work," says Ayana. She did a project on Hughes last year.

James's hand is up. "I marked where he sort of lets you inside his mind with this image of the mirror. And the transition is pretty smooth, too," and James reads aloud: "'I have thought about that team meeting to select escorts often since 1966. But after talking to Greg, I've thought about it in a new way. Now, a mirror is part of the memory, a mirror in which I see a reflection of myself. I am ashamed of what I see.'"

"That's cool," Jenna agrees. "He's *reflecting*, and he uses this mirror image. And farther down that paragraph where he says how he was passive, I like how he uses the sound of *something* and *nothing*: 'I was passive. Let's just see what happens, I thought. The something that happened was that nothing happened.'"

"So even though that paragraph is reflection, not so much story action or dialogue, both you and James noticed it because Romano did stuff with sound and image and structure, right?" I'd been listing on the board as we talked:

> storytelling—scene, characters, dialogue
>
> time shifts—story from past memory, years later, right now as telling the story
>
> reflections on self and on story's meaning—through image, poetry allusion, sound

Arguing from Personal Experience

"Aside from the poetry allusion, these are all techniques you've used in your earlier pieces, right? In the profile or the zone piece or Holden's narrative. And in your most recent argument about Fugard's ending, you were quoting dialogue as evidence and were reflecting on the meaning of the characters' relationship and their story. How many of you think you might have a true story to tell and reflect on that argues for taking a stand on something you believe in, rather than 'countenancing' something you see as wrong?" Long pause. "Or maybe you actually saw someone else take a stand, take that risk, and you thought 'I could do that too?'" Another pause. Then some hands go up. "Okay, let's open our notebooks, close our eyes, and just think back for a while. If a true story like that, a personal experience, starts to come into your memory, you could begin jotting it down. Seeing what you remember. . . ."

Rethinking My Assignment: Offering Options

I scribble in my own notebook for five minutes. When I look around, only about half the class seems to have started. I decide it might be helpful—interesting, even—to offer an option. "How many of you know what issue you want to write about?" Almost all the hands go up. So it's the *story* that's the problem for some of them, maybe just thinking of one or going public with it.

"Of course, you could argue for your cause *without* using a whole story, couldn't you? You could make a list of reasons why you care about this particular cause, why it's important to you to stand up for it, what risks might be involved. You could include reasons for and against why the issue matters, but you'd *subordinate* the reasons against it—making your argument the way you did in your paragraph about the ending of *"Master Harold,"* right? How many of you think you might like to take this approach rather than start with the storytelling?" Five or six hands go up. Then a few more. "All right. I'll post these two options [see Figure 4.2] to the online conference later today so you can get a draft ready for tomorrow. You're not shooting for anything as long as Romano's piece. What do you think, can you make your case in two pages?" They nod. "You've already got some criteria for writing argument from our last piece. Would you like to exchange drafts in class tomorrow to get some ideas of what others are doing? And then we'll be in a better place to firm up our lists of criteria for revising and assessing."

Critique/Criteria: Which Comes First?

The next day I ask to hear what issues students chose to write about, what they want to protest. We make a list on the board: homophobia, racism, anti-Semitism, bullying, abortion, anti-abortion, evolution (and creationism) being taught in schools, child abuse, gender inequities in team sports. It turns out that the class split pretty equally between storytelling/reflection and straight argument, so in pairing them up for peer response I try to mix the approaches. "I haven't made official response sheets for you since we're not sure yet about criteria, but let's give feedback on how well the writer's particular approach seems to be working—that is, storytelling/reflection or argument. So on your first read, mark where and why the writing is holding

1. Draft and type up for class a roughly two-page piece about a time when you or someone you know stood up for something you believe in, even when others did not stand up for it. **Bring this scene to life with description and a little dialogue. Show us** what went on inside you—reasons, feelings—**and reflect on** why this belief and this story are important to you. As you draft, keep in mind the techniques we saw Romano using in his article.

OR

2. Draft—and type up for class—a roughly two-page piece about an issue important enough to you to take a stand. **Admitting why** the issue might be controversial, **explain** why it matters to you, some ways you could take a stand, and some risks of doing so. As you draft, keep in mind the arguing you did in your debate and paragraphs on the ending of *"Master Harold"*—how you **organized your points around a thesis sentence, subordinated less important to more important, incorporated examples, and used subordination.**

FIGURE 4.2. TWO OPTIONS FOR MAKING A CASE.

your interest and where it gets dull. On your second reading, annotate suggestions for things your partner might add, cut, or change to hold your interest better. Remember how you listed what Romano did to 'put you there' in his experience and his head—and also what questions you, as reader, hoped he would answer? Try to apply that process to your reading of your partner's draft, because even the straight argument approach will be personal, and you'll want to get inside the writer's thoughts and feelings about the issue. When both partners finish, you can have a conversation about the suggestions, but keep it quiet, or go out in the hall."

When the students all return to the circle, we talk a bit about the two approaches, why they chose the one they did, what they liked in the way their partners used the other approach. Many students say they liked reading the stories best. Some who told stories explain that they did so because it seemed more fun; a few say they couldn't think of a story at the time, but now they can.

"So, Ms. Michaels, can we change over tonight?" asks Garret. "I thought of a story I could use."

I'm thrilled that Garret's actually asking to revise, though I carefully avoid using the *R* word when I assure him that yes, this is fine.

Sydney says, "I think Jenna sort of combined the two ways, I mean the story and the arguments. She has these two little scenes—no dialogue, just sort of moments, that make it seem real, but then she gives facts to back up her opinion about abortion. I think I want to make mine more like that."

"Jenna, would you mind reading yours aloud, so we get what Sydney's talking about?"

Jenna reads:

Last year when my mom and I were driving in the car on the way to my ballet lesson we passed by a house with a large sign hanging from its front window. The sign read: **Make Abortion Illegal!** This got my mom and I started on a conversation about abortion; our beliefs and ideas on the subject. We both agreed: the issue of abortion should always be up to the mother and should be legal. You never know the circumstances and it does differ but I believe it's her body and it shouldn't be up to anyone else what to do with it. Some people are "pro life" but although I am saddened just by the idea of killing a baby, it's not really a baby yet. There are two kinds of abortion. The first kind is performed early on in the pregnancy and it is only taking medications that kill the egg. The second form is a little more grotesque. This is used only later in pregnancy, if it's discovered the baby has Down syndrome, is mentally retarded or has a fatal disease, it can be killed even though it has already formed. Although this doesn't appeal to me, I still believe that the mother should always have a choice.

I remember specifically one time in class when we got into the topic of abortion. A lot of the boys in my class thought that abortion should be illegal. This really upset me. They don't have anything to do with abortion. They're not ever going to be pregnant and they don't have to worry. Men can easily walk away from a relationship with a child and it happens all the time. I'm not saying that every man is going to do this, but they do walk away from relationships more than women do. I'm never going to attack people's opinions because I respect them, but I will defend my belief on any subject. And on the subject of abortion my belief is that no matter the circumstance, the woman should always have a choice.

"I like how she starts out with her and her mom in the car discussing it," Jessica explains, "because that's where you often have good talks with people—in the car, going some place. It helps me get into the paper. And I like the real-life class discussion with the boys."

"Yeah, but she's not fair to the fathers," Brooks says. "It's their baby too."

"Well, is there some strategy Jenna could use to deal with Brooks's objection?" I ask.

"I think a statistic, if she could get one, to show it's not just her *opinion* but that guys really do walk out a lot of the time when they get the girl pregnant," Connor suggests equably. "She just says it happens *all the time*, and that men don't have anything to do with abortion. But some guys help pay for it and—I mean, maybe you need to point that out, so you'll sound more fair."

"Does that sound useful, Jenna? Now you can think about Brooks as one of your readers and really try to address his comment—which you do, to some extent, already, where you said that *not* every man walks away from relationships. But think about Connor's suggestion as a strategy in your argument. One other thing you might want to get into more specifically is what *risks* you'd be willing to take to defend your opinion. You say you won't attack other people's opinions, out of respect, but that you'll *defend* yours. What does that mean, exactly? Can you imagine a situation where speaking up for a woman's right to have an abortion could get you in trouble? Or, to go further: Can you imagine a situation where, say, you'd be asked to go beyond arguing? Suppose a friend asked you to help her get an abortion, for instance. Or even just to go with her to the clinic. How might that test your beliefs? And if you were to help her, what risks might you run? How might you feel? I'm not saying what you should or shouldn't do, but just pushing for clarification, because "defending an opinion" could mean a lot of different things, right?"

"Yeah, I guess. That's really hard to think about. I guess it would make a difference *why* she wanted the abortion."

"Now that you've all read your partner's approach, and you've heard Jenna's, I wonder whether we could make a short list of criteria that would work for everybody—that is, for *both* approaches, including Jen's Chinese menu mix. Doesn't it seem that you're all doing essentially the same thing? Arguing for some kind of intervention to support a personal belief or value, but just using different techniques? What do you want your reader to 'get' from your piccc?"

Peter says, "To agree with me that my issue really matters—it's not just for the sake of arguing. And it's not just for me but because it's about basic fairness that everybody should care about. And . . . well, how even though one person can't change everything, it's like that story about the kid rescuing some of the starfish on the beach—he can't save them all, but it makes a difference for the ones he does save."

"Ooo, I like that, about the starfish. Can I use that in my piece?" Julia asks.

"Sure, I guess," Peter tells her. "It's just some story Ms. Skvir told us in class the other day."

"So, Peter, can you translate your comment into some criteria?" I ask. "Or can somebody else help him out?"

By the end of this discussion, we have three items on the board. The writer should:

1. make the issue feel important—personally and for the reader
2. use a good mix of facts and feelings, generalizations and details
3. use selected approaches well, with wording and organization that sustain the reader's interest

The wording is mine, but the ideas represent class consensus. I send them off to spend one more night on the draft, with a reminder to keep reading it *aloud* as they work and *to keep their readers in mind*. I'm not expecting a polished piece in the time we have available; the process matters more—the learning that's been going on.

The Revisions: What I Learn

When the revised drafts come in, no single piece rises to the top: Connor's, on bullying, exhibits clear reasoning but the writing is flat; it would benefit from a personal story. Jess's, also on bullying, tells an arresting story but her reflections on it are limited. More practice will help most of the class combine the two approaches. However, certain students who'd been quiet during our discussion of Romano's article surprise me with the urgency of their writing: Jessica, for instance, expressing a passionate belief that "just as it would be a monumental step for our country to have its first black president, so I believe that one day gay marriage will be legal in every single state, even though now that is unimaginable." From this piece, I learn that Jessica has joined the school's Gay/Straight Alliance and plans to participate in GSA conventions at other schools. She vows, "Every time I hear a derogatory term for gays used, I will say something." For Jessica to "say something" confrontational is about the equivalent of marching into clouds of tear gas.

I'm surprised to read an admission from smooth, witty James, the journalist, that last summer he found himself wanting in courage when his tent mates at camp teased a homesick camper. By not standing up for this kid, he says, he lost self-respect. Next day he apologized but worries that his tent mate didn't believe he felt sorry. Next time, he thinks he'll act differently.

Jordan has written about the stories his family has told him of the Civil Rights era protests. He imagines himself participating in marches and going to jail:

> My dad always shares this story of when he and his friends would have a basketball game in an Italian neighborhood. In the league my dad's team would beat them and after every game the Italians would chase them back to their neighborhood. My grandparents tell me stories of how they weren't allowed to eat at certain restaurants because it was for whites only. Hearing that really bothers me and makes me want to stand up for them. . . . Whites were allowed many more opportunities and the part that bothers me the most is that the people that were running our country were supporting Segregation. They were taking away our Civil Rights, but we had many Civil Rights Activists in our corner. Such as Dr. Martin Luther King Jr., Malcolm X, Rosa Parks, Rev. Jesse Jackson, and many others. I wish I were there to stand up against this system of government with the other pioneers. They were true warriors that believed in equal rights, and if I were around then I would try my absolute best to help. I would be marching for our laws to be fair.

This is the best writing I've seen from Jordan so far—direct, specific, forceful. Clearly, it's important to offer kids a variety of topics and approaches. I also need to remind myself that even the quietest, most seemingly detached students in the class can have strong feelings about some of the subjects under discussion—feelings they may be more comfortable writing than speaking. Jordan ends his piece with an optimistic view of race relations that the upcoming election seems to be inspiring in many of my students, regardless of their race. He writes: "After all of these warriors' hard work, look at how diverse this country has become. An African American man may become President of the United States of America, and not only that, many schools are diverse with all different races. This shows how united we have become as a country and as people, and that is an outstanding accomplishment." While I know Jordan has come up against racial inequities that some of his classmates have only heard or read about, he's still capable of these moments of exhilaration and faith in the future. His writing voice here is authentic, though he has other voices as well, I think, that haven't yet emerged clearly on paper.

So Far/What Next?

Storytelling. Self-examination. Argument. I think the students have developed an interest in the range of possibilities that writing offers. And they're becoming aware of the complex mix of processes it entails: remembering, imagining, reflecting, discovery of purpose, gathering of supporting details and evidence, shaping for public consumption. With this respect has come an interest in one another's writing and an ability to talk about it. Many of the kids are becoming better listeners to one another's voices, both in discussion and on paper. They're learning to read as writers, write as readers. And—which is crucial if the free-choice project is to succeed—they're gradually discovering what they like best to write and where their strengths lie.

But I want to add poetry to their repertoire. Later, in spring, we'll do the traditional poetry unit and write seven or eight poems, building a portfolio, but just now I want to look at a handful of poems that can offer us a new way to journey—poems that will not only continue our study of the journey in literature but also invite us to sharpen our senses, explore new kinds of structures, and begin to think using metaphor.

Chapter 5

A Taste of Poetry

Nov. 30—Watching Galway drag his wet, smelly stuffed bear around the room. Heard his fierce hunting growl, all the way from other end of the house. He licks it, loves it, then bites it, kicks it.

Dec. 2—*Nearly bald, this stuffed bear*
was/is meant for my (small?) niece to cuddle
against cancer, but now she's well,
my fierce coon cat inherits.
Bear becomes prey and infant/kitten,
licked, stroked, chewed, kicked, torn.
From the next room I hear the hunter's
growl. Bear's sparse fur is wet/soaked
with saliva, stinks of cat breath. His head/snout's
a perfect fit for a cat's jaw/mouth
and what a lovely/lively arc he makes/when Galway
when Galway lofts him/it into
unresisting air to catch it in his teeth.
Cancer loved my niece and me like this,
held us by the scruff of the neck to give
long, hot licks till we were bald
and limp as newborns, dragged us
from room to room till finally some new
toy offered it a better game.

Dec. 10—revising

Bear Game

Nearly bald, this stuffed bear
was meant for my small niece to cuddle
against cancer, but now she's well
my fierce coon cat inherits.
Bear becomes prey and kitten—
licked, stroked, chewed, kicked, torn.
From the next room I hear the hunter's
growl. Bear's sparse fur is soaked
in saliva, stinks of cat's breath. His snout's
a perfect fit for a cat's mouth,
and what a lively arc when Galway
lofts him into glittering air
to catch him in his teeth. Cancer
loved Heather and me like this,
seized us by the scruff of the neck
to give long, hot licks till we were
bald and limp as newborns,
dragged us from room to room till
finally some new toy offered it
a better game.

From my notebook

Commentary

I wrote this poem several years ago, starting from the little prose entry about my cat at play, which I'd jotted down with no specific expectations. It felt like snapping a casual picture. Seeing a poem take shape on the page a couple of days later took me by surprise, particularly its turn from cat to cancer. Not intentional. A little creepy, in fact, the cancer cat. And I would not have chosen to portray myself as a victim.

But the sequence—prose quickwrite into drafts of a poem—turned out to offer a helpful model for my students. I don't show it to them until we've read some other poets' work; I want mine to be just one more sample, not privileged by virtue of its being their teacher's. I hasten to assure them that there is no single "right" way for a poem to take shape, any more than an essay or story has to start from an outline bristling with Roman numerals. I've had new poems grow line by line in my head while I was out jogging. When this happens, I have to say the lines again and again out loud, memorizing and revising till I can get back to the house and grab a pencil. I've written on napkins in cafés and while riding on a bus, surrounded by shrieking kids. The point is, students too often encounter *finished* poems, pristine on the pages of a textbook, looking as remote as crown jewels under glass and followed by study questions about the poet's intended meaning. They need to see and to hear real, live people making poetry, crossing out words, messing with line breaks, discovering meaning but respecting mysteries, and, above all, surrendering to the unexpected. They need to find out for themselves the truth of Robert Frost's "No surprise for the writer? No surprise for the reader." The turns and leaps that a good poem usually takes on its journey as images morph from literal to figurative and one word leads to another through sound and association—not necessarily logic or conventional syntax—can help student writers trust their own imaginations, their own powers of associative thinking, and the discovery of idea through metaphor. Poet Billy Collins says in his introduction to *180 More: Extraordinary Poems for Every Day*, "Each poem can be a ride from a place we recognize to a place beyond definition—from a glass ashtray on a table to the mountain of ashes that is the past" (xxi). But too often in a classroom the Meaning of this ride—the single correct meaning—becomes the only thing that matters.

Many high school students enter ninth grade having encountered no poetry since their grade school experiences with Dr. Seuss, haiku, or Shel Silverstein. I ask mine to write down whatever they can remember of their encounters with poetry. Some have struggled with writing assignments that are really decontextualized prompts directing them to dash off a spring poem or a poem with four colors in it. Some have dutifully memorized the definitions of *simile* and *alliteration* and labeled figures of speech in worksheets or engaged in analyses of "what the poet is trying to say." Many have never heard—or have never read—a poem aloud.

Unfolding a Poem: As Reader and Writer

I want to demystify and re-mystify poetry for my ninth graders. We did share a poem out loud on the first day of class, Naomi Shihab Nye's "Eye-to-Eye," with each of us reading a line, building the poem together. Then we read it again, trying to follow the cues the poem offered us—the syntax, repetitions and contrasts, line breaks and punctuation. Now, introducing poetry as a genre for my students to experience as *writers*, I want them to hear and see a poem actually unfolding, rather than as a whole, completed piece. I also plan to invite them to consider how the ways in which a poem proceeds might be comparable—or not—to the operations of a profile, a description, and a story, the genres they've already written. I choose to begin with Mark Doty's "Charlie Howard's Descent": partly because it unfolds its narrative and reflection gradually, its four-line stanzas sometimes continuing a sentence into the next stanza (enjambing), sometimes ending a sentence in mid-stanza; and partly because its subject, the forming of a gay man's identity and his murder by teenage boys, not only offers another lens through which to view our year's theme of the personal journey but also takes us back to an issue we hadn't explored much in *Catcher in the Rye*—Holden's view of "flits" and his fear that Mr. Antolini has made a pass at him when Holden was staying the night at his former teacher's apartment.

I ask the students whether a poem can tell a story. Can it present different characters? Action? Sure, they tell me—"Green Eggs and Ham" or Sarah Stout who refuses to take the garbage out. Can a poem leave you wondering? Can it make you feel something? Can it make a point? Somebody mentions Langston Hughes—"that one with the raisin in the sun . . . you know, the dream that explodes. I guess it does all those things." Someone else mentions Shel Silverstein's "Homework" poem. Is there anything you *couldn't* write a poem about, I ask them. Silence. And then, in spite of our accumulating evidence, the usual: "Oh, it's mostly gotta be about spring. Or death."

I hand out Mark Doty's poem, face down and folded over so that when students turn it up, only the first stanza will be visible. "Okay, turn it over. I'm going to read you this poem, one stanza at a time, so we can see how Mark Doty paces the story and helps us make some guesses about where it's going. One thing I'll ask you to watch and listen for in particular, and that's how certain objects—*real, literal objects*—take on new meanings, new weight, like a snowball gathering more snow. They become *metaphors—figurative*, not literal. [I know from past experience that many of my ninth graders will be familiar with *figures of speech* but not with the terms *literal* and *figurative*.] These objects, these metaphors, may affect how you feel about the events and characters." Then I read the title aloud: "Charlie Howard's Descent."

"So, any expectations the title raises for you? Remember how you discussed the chapter titles you made up for *Catcher*? The kinds of titles you agreed you liked best? What about Mark Doty's title?"

"So there's this guy, Charlie. Like he's the main character," says Brooks. "And he descends. He has some kind of bad thing happen to him?"

"Some kind of fall?" suggests Peter. "Or like going down to the Underworld."

"So maybe it's going to be scary," Garret says hopefully.

"Okay, see how a title can get you wondering? And also give you key facts you'll need to know? Always start with the title—as a reader, that is. As a writer—well, I often can't figure out my title till I've written a bunch of drafts. Now, let's start the journey through this poem. Listen up." And I read aloud:

> *Between the bridge and the river*
> *he falls through*
> *a huge portion of night;*
> *it is not as if falling*

"And then there's a stanza break—a lot of white space. You might think of it as visual art, both the picture he's making for you with words—in your mind—and the way the stanza actually looks on the page. Any questions you're wondering about? Any predictions? Any particular feel to the piece so far?"

The students notice the feeling of height, the scariness of falling "through night," the way the first line sets up a picture of the distance "between," the gap, which seems scary, and how just those three words in the second line make you feel the "falling through," make you really pay attention to it, slow down, like you're falling in slow motion. One girl asks if he's committing suicide. Why is the night a "huge portion" I wonder aloud, "like a portion of food he's had handed out to him, like he can't choose?" I want them to see me wonder, speculate, ask the poem questions. I try to avoid asking the students for "meaning" so that they can do their own wondering as the story gets told. But I do try to help them hear the poem in relation to other genres and to their own experience. For instance, I ask whether this opening is any different from the way a novel or short story—a prose piece—might describe a setting.

"Yeah," Jess says. "It's not, like, a whole big paragraph of details. But the ones he does put in make you feel things. It makes you slow way down. So it's not just details about what a place looks like. It seems like more than just facts."

Several people are nodding. I add, "And it also works for me kind of like a piece of music, with different instruments, different sounds. That word *huge*—that echoes the word *through*: it *sounds* and therefore *feels* HUGE. The long *u* sound and the soft *g* and the effort to make the *h*—it takes a while to say it. It's not just big or large, but huge." I want to get students listening for patterns of sound and how these help create feeling. Since they can't see more than four lines at a time, they have little choice but to focus in close— as they did when copying and responding to their passages from *Catcher*. But, unlike discussing something they've already read, here they're curious to go on reading, to see what happens. I want them also to read as poets— to be curious about how, in the brief space of a poem, Mark Doty will find ways to make what happens matter.

"It's like suspense is building," Nick says cheerfully.

"It seems like he's not going to rush the story," Peter says. "He uses *falling* twice, and it seems like the next stanza's going to kind of explain what the fall *isn't*, before anything more happens."

"So let's see if Peter's right. You can fold down the next stanza and pick up from the previous line—"it is not as if falling"

is something new. Over and over
he slipped into the gulf
between what he knew and how
he was known. What others wanted

"Ooh," says Julia. "So he's tried to kill himself before now. Over and over. Um . . . but I don't get the last part."

"Yes, that's pretty interesting," and I pick up my pencil. "I'm going to mark those lines so I can come back to think about them some more. Is there some gulf—some big space—between what you know and how other people know you? And is this maybe part of the story? What do you think the poem's doing here?"

"It's filling in the character. I mean, his past. And the last sentence that's going into the next stanza—well, it seems like how other people see this guy or want him to be really matters," James suggests. "So maybe he hasn't tried to kill himself over and over but just had to live with people not liking him. Not accepting him."

In the next few stanzas, we find out that people in stores and restaurants laughed at his "gestures," his "limp wrists," his earrings, but that because he can't "live with one hand tied behind his back," he "began to fall / into the star-faced section / of night between the trestle / and the water." By this point, certain kids are saying maybe the "falling" isn't a suicidal leap but more of a falling into deep depression "because people want him to be someone he's not," James says. Then the narrator shifts from third person to a reflective, interpretive "I," who speculates:

> *I imagine he took the insults in*
> *and made of them a place to live;*
> *we learn to use the names*
> *because they are there,*
>
> *familiar furniture:* faggot
> *was the bed he slept in, hard*
> *and white, but simple somehow,*
> queer *something sharp*
>
> *but finally useful, a tool,*
> *all the jokes a chair,*
> *stiff-backed to keep the spine straight,*
> *a table, a lamp. . . .*

The students don't comment on the shift from "he" to "I" until I wonder out loud about it, but once I do, Julia says that it's not just "I"—there's a "we." And that the "we" makes us *all* part of the prejudice, the name-calling.

"That's interesting. I hadn't thought about it, but now I'm wondering—do you think shifting to the 'I' makes it *easier* to move on to the 'we'? I mean, if the narrator's staying in the background, saying 'he' and 'they' and then suddenly saying 'we all use the insults this way,' it might seem like a pretty sudden shift and maybe preachy, but with the 'I' first, he sounds like he's trying to figure something out for himself about Charlie—'I imagine'—and that reflection leads him on to the 'we,' including himself."

I've lost some of them, but that's okay. Others are nodding, and at least they all see I'm figuring things out along with them—I'm not the answer key. Also, they want to go on to the next stanza. They're hooked. Ayana points us to the way the insults become Charlie's "home," his "furniture." "Is that what you meant," she asks, "about how the objects—the chairs and the bed and the lamp—get more important, because they're the insults he lives with? They mean more than just furniture?"

Before I can agree, Jessica, who wrote a piece about standing up for gay rights, shoots her hand up. "So it's really bad, because the insults are making him see himself as no good, but the poem says those words, like *queer*, are 'useful tools.' And that's why he's falling, over and over."

"Yeah!" Jenna agrees. "That's the gap between the bridge and the water, maybe. That line you said you were marking, back, where is it? Oh, here—the gap between what he knows 'and how he was known.'"

We finish reading the poem. The kids had pictured Charlie as a teenage boy but then discover he's "fallen for twenty-three years." It's the three boys who push him off the bridge who are teenagers, "really boys now, afraid, / their fathers' cars shivering behind them, headlights on." Some of the students are baffled that Charlie, after his death, "climbs back" out of the river and tells the boys:

> *It's all right, that he knows*
> *they didn't believe him*
> *when he said he couldn't swim,*
> *and blesses his killers*
>
> *in the way that only the dead*
> *can afford to forgive.*

"I wouldn't forgive those jerks," says Nick.

"Well, you aren't dead," Connor retorts. "It says that nobody *living* 'can afford to forgive.'"

"I wonder why they pushed him off?" I ask.

"Because there were three of them," says Jess. "They probably were drinking or something. And bored. And really dumb."

"Uh, maybe they're kind of scared of older gay men—like Holden was," Matt suggests.

"It's the name-calling where it all starts," Jessica asserts. "It makes them forget he's a real person. He's just a label."

"What name did Holden use? What was the term back in the 1940s and '50s?" I remind them. I want to give them some background information on homosexuality that might help them think about how Matt is connecting the poem to the novel.

"Oh, *flit*," Jordan says, laughing a little.

"Yes. Do you remember how nervous he is about flits—because he says guys have come on to him at his various boarding schools? And how he argues with himself after he leaves Mr. Antolini's apartment that night be-cause he really respects and likes this teacher and doesn't want to think that he was making a pass at him if he really wasn't? Back then, homosexuality was classified as a neurosis by psychiatrists, and if you were gay you were supposed to get psychiatric help so you could become 'normal.' So Holden also uses the word *pervert* about gays. The medical classification of homo-sexuality as a perversion wasn't dropped till the early 1960s, and the move-ment for gay rights didn't really get going till the '70s. One of the stereo-types about gay men was that they were dangerous—that they 'preyed on' boys. Do you think what happens to Charlie Howard is fictional? Or a true story? And would that make a difference in how you react to it?"

The students argue a bit. For most, it "feels real" (someone mentions "that guy in Wyoming," Matt Shepard), except for the part about Charlie blessing his killers after he's dead. "That's not something a writer could know about a dead person. You'd *have* to make it up," says Ayana, "But I don't think it matters to me if it really happened or not. As long as it feels real in the poem."

"Actually, it's a true story," I tell them, "but I didn't know that the first time I read it. There's a footnote at the end, saying the killing took place in Bangor, Maine, in 1984. If you were to read it in a newspaper, would it be told this way?"

"Nope," says James. "It would start by identifying him and giving dates and places—all the facts. And no fancy description, like the huge night, or whatever it was. And no stanzas. Oh yeah, and no metaphors, like the furni-ture."

"I think a news story could have metaphors," says Connor, my other newsman, "especially an editorial. But maybe the 'I' that imagines what the name-calling was like for Charlie would be from interviews—the way news stories quote people's opinions."

"Oh, the way you used quotes in your profiles?" I ask. "So something like: 'Mark Doty, a close friend of the deceased, says . . .'"

"I can't imagine those lines about, you know, the slurs being like the furniture of Charlie's mind, being in a newspaper," says Ayana. "Anyway, I like it better as a poem. I can really *see* those scared boys and the headlights and what their parents will say."

The bell has rung and students are cramming binders into backpacks, but Julia stays behind to tell me, "That was a totally amazing poem!"

Visiting Poet

While it's important to help students see and hear and wonder at a poem unfolding on the page as they read or listen, it may be even more crucial for them to experience discovery and surprise as a poem of their *own* takes shape. For some, the prospect of writing a poem can feel overwhelming—what to write about, how to start, how to decide whether to rhyme, where to break stanzas and lines if they're not using rhyme or meter, how to "put in" figures of speech. I may show them my "Bear Game" poem at this point so they can see one way of starting—from a notebook entry and a specific object and situation. I may talk about some options I perceived and discarded as I drafted—why I rejected using stanzas, for instance, or trying out a traditional form such as a sonnet. ("Bear Game" has a sonnet-like "turn" about two-thirds of the way through but none of the conventional rhyme schemes or iambic pentameter.) I might discuss why I used certain words and phrases from the original notebook entry and how I kept reading aloud as I drafted the poem because that not only helped me hear where to break lines and change words for better sounds but also seemed to keep ideas and feelings flowing.

But the kids need to meet a live poet who's *not* their daily teacher. So I like to bring in a visiting poet early in the writing process, preferably someone of a different age, gender, or race than mine. This person needn't be from outside the school, though when we have the money, I do invite an established poet to spend several days working in all the ninth- and tenth-grade classes. One can find poets through a state arts council, or through writers-in-the-schools programs; I've invited poets I meet when I give or take workshops and attend writing conferences. But another teacher, or a student's parent, or one of our alumni—or even a talented twelfth grader— can be an effective guest artist, depending on the strength and accessibility of their work and their ability to connect with teenagers. This year we have a new poet in our department, a young woman who's studied in Oregon with Dorianne Laux and whose sample class, a poetry workshop, impressed me when she came to interview. I invite her to give this workshop to my students.

Kate Westhaver talks to the kids about why she writes poetry: that it's a love–hate relationship because it makes her think but also confuses and scares her. She says that she reads a lot of poems—in books, magazines, online—and hears them at live readings and slams, but sometimes these poems baffle her. "And I think that's okay," she says. "I can still enjoy a poem even when it confuses me. It's okay to not understand, not 'get' every line. Sometimes I just enjoy the sounds, or maybe certain lines speak to me." For her, writing a poem has an element of play. "If I let go of making sense, I can enjoy making sound. The music of the poem can inspire random beauty and surprising connections for me. Things I didn't know I knew. Lines that make me wonder, 'gee, how did I come up with this?'"

Kate hands out copies of E. E. Cummings's "anyone lived in a pretty how town." I'm happy that we have another "story poem" here—another life "journey," though a somewhat different one from "Charlie Howard's Descent"—and one that offers both mystery and music. Definitely, as Kate said about her own writing, it contains lines that will make us wonder, "How did he come up with that?" She asks us to listen with pencils in hand as we take turns reading the stanzas aloud. "Mark lines that you like and moments you [f]urprising, including rhymes, capitalization, and punctuation." And a [poi]nt begins:

anyone lived in a pretty how town
(with up so floating many bells down)
spring summer autumn winter
he sang his didn't he danced his did

[W]hen the reading ends, students have discovered some new options [f]or their own poems: varying refrains, off-rhymes mixed with true rhymes, four-beat lines, the absence of punctuation and capitalization, and a whole new take on language—or, to use a word most of them don't know—*syntax*. The poem shakes up a lot of their assumptions about writing, let alone writing poetry. But they seem to agree with Kate that one can enjoy a poem even—or especially?—when it confuses them. And they love the refrains: the varied order of the four seasons and of the "sun moon stars rain." Kids pick out other favorite lines—"how children are apt to forget to remember" and the whole idea of "no one" being in love with "anyone." They wonder what a "how town" is, what it means to sow your isn't or dance your did, and they agree that "up so floating many bells down" may not make sense but it's got "a feeling."

Garret's looking worried. "I like it, but it doesn't mean anything, does it?"

"I like it because it seems like this sad love poem," Jen says. "'No one' loves 'anyone' so much that she 'laughed his joy and cried his grief,' and then when he dies she kisses his face. And they're buried side by side. That's true love."

"Yeah, but," says Peter, "if you put capital letters on them, they'd be characters, but with lowercase, it could be that *nobody* loves this guy—I mean, like in the second stanza it says women and men 'cared for anyone not at all.' So that makes it really sad. Like a love poem with no love in it?"

Kate avoids doing what Billy Collins describes as "tying a poem to a chair and beating it with a rubber hose." She invites us to go on thinking about the poem on our own and moves us into her writing exercise. First, she invites us to get up, stretch, and find new seats. Then she has us each divide a sheet of paper into quarters, number them, and listen to four excerpts from four pieces of music that she has on her iPod. She tells us that listening to music often gets her started writing a poem. "Do any of you do homework to music? What music fosters creativity for you?" she asks them. As we begin to listen, we're to write whatever comes into our pencil, no censoring, just keep the pencil moving—"whatever words the music brings to you. Don't worry about writing sentences or making sense. Don't consciously try to write about the music, to describe it or analyze it. Just let the words come while the music plays. Just let go of making sense. Stay silent even between the excerpts, and shake out your hand if you need to at those breaks."

I write along with the class, but I also jot reminders to myself of what kinds of music Kate has chosen—just my impressions, though I do want to get titles from her later on: "1. very soft strings, grave, formal music;

2. pipe flute breath very Eastern; 3. percussive log drum; 4. a mix of vocal and instrumental, soprano hum on the ah vowel with jazzy scat style."

Kate invites students up to the board to record favorite words or word combinations from their writing. The board fills up fast:

quicksilver	chaos
electric	gravestones
enormous	magical
toy store	Audrey Hepburn
stomp	smoking cigarettes
choke	up
ambience	down
electrocute	tribal drums
Arabian market	sirens
African jungle	mall muzak
bongos	nurse's office
boom box	music
sparkles	elevator music
drown out	sleepy
clowns	ticktock.

Then we get an assignment: "Steal any four words or phrases you like from the board along with material from your own writing and create at least ten lines of poetry. You can change, manipulate, any of this material and also add new things." The kids are excited. Some are already starting before Kate has finished giving directions.

We haven't established any criteria for assessing these poems. I don't plan to grade them or even write comments at this stage. But the next day volunteers read their pieces aloud, and after applause or finger snapping, I ask readers to say at least one thing they like about their own piece. At times, I expand on these comments: "Yes, Sarah, the way you used that refrain made the feeling of the speaker go deeper, for me, anyway. And it gave the poem a structure—like a song. That's a technique others of you might want to try." As we go around the circle and hear each writer's comment, I ask for volunteers who can remind us of anything *else* from that particular poem. I want the students to realize they don't need a copy of the poem in front of them to respond to hearing it. The kind and manner of response may be different when we work from memory—more spontaneous, more tentative, more visceral and less analytical. It could be as simple as "Could you read that first part over again? It had some words I really liked the sounds of." Gradually, if we listen to enough poems together this way, the students will find they can experience a poem more fully—notice and remember, feel more.

James's poem starts out with all the distractions that were keeping him from responding to the music as he wrote: the teacher interrupting with more directions, the ticking clock, his hand getting tired. He asks, "how to escape this aggravating ambience?" And then in answering his question, he finds language and line breaks that put us in the moment:

> I turn on the boom box of my mind
> And turn up the volume until it can't go any
> Higher. The music sparkles in, drowning her out
> My thoughts clear up

James says he especially likes these last four lines because of the boom box image for his mind and the phrase "music sparkles in," which he says is just the way it felt. He also likes the way he used spacing in the last line to slow it down, to show that's the way it happened. Julia tells him that it makes a good ending.

In her own poem, Julia likes the way she combined words from a recent science lesson on the structure of the ear with some of the images she "heard" in the music. Other kids enjoy the surprise of this combination, too, and several tell her that the *b* alliteration makes the ending image "really cool." She's asked to read the poem again:

> Shards of quicksilver
> Magically showering through
> The ear canal
> Electrocuting each labyrinth
> With mesmerizing waves of
> Arabian nights
>
> And dense African jungles
> Sprouting for the cartilage

Spreading lushly
Into the auditory canal

Ear drums keeping the beat
Of the bongos.

"Julia, any idea what led you to think of using words from your science book?"

"Well, . . ." She thinks for a moment. "Maybe because I'd just spent a lot of time listening to Ms. Westhaver's music, so that made me think about listening in general, and ears and so on."

"And that led to your pun on eardrums! Which makes a wonderful ending. The whole poem sounds like someone having fun, doesn't it? So many of the words are fun to say. Any of you remember specific words from the poem? Or some of those verbs that are so full of energy you can almost feel them in your own body?" Kids mention *electrocute, labyrinth, mesmerize, sprout, lushly, keep the beat.* Julia's beaming. It's fun to hear your own poem given back to you—fun to know you made an impression on your listeners.

Garret wrote about listening to his hungry stomach's music "rambling and growling" along with a radio's jungle drums as he doodled on paper. Kids tell him they like having the three things rambling along together—the growls, the drum, and the doodles. Sarah writes about three different kinds of music, including "elevator music / that takes me down / but never up" and country music "yawling and drawling / 'bout hillbilly horses." She gets applause for the rhyme and for the idea of elevator music as a "downer." Jessica, often so matter-of-fact, finds herself writing of "clowns walking to their gravestones" and a mountain that "invites me to join him / trembling in the dark." Ayana is shy about reading hers, but finally we coax it out of her, and the class is already applauding halfway through. Something inside Ayana has let loose!

Not that cheesy mall muzik
But tribal drum beats
Cries for a revolution
War paint
Ring of sirens.
Red and blue lites

Pulsed through my frame
Eyes bloodshot
Brain goin'
Non-stop

Classy?
Smokin Hepburn cigs in
Cocktails?
KRAZY!
Smokin' Marlboros in
Neon jumpsuits

Rising from that
Xtasy koma.
An animal in the morning.
That rave . . .
Fresh in my mind

Party at 7th?
It'll be krazy.
I'll be an animal in the morning.

We discuss what writing these poems felt like. Students volunteer that at first it was hard because they were "trying to fit these words together that didn't make sense." But then they remembered that Ms. Westhaver had said it didn't have to make sense—that they should "let go of trying to make sense and just have fun." And that helped.

"So might there be different *kinds* of sense—and different ways our minds can make them?" I ask.

"Maybe. Yeah, I think so," Peter agrees. "I think some of these poems do make sense—like Ayana's. Really, all of them do, maybe. They're just not things we'd normally write. They kind of show ways our minds can behave when we let them break rules."

"So can any of you come up with some rules you broke?" I ask. Gradually the students mention writing without whole sentences, using no punctuation or caps, making a line with just one word in it or leaving lots of spaces between words. What made them break these "rules"? Most said, "Because it felt right. Because it made the poem better." A few allowed as how they hadn't even noticed they were breaking rules. No one mentions putting words together to make unusual or "impossible" images and situations, but I think that's what they meant when they said they worried about not making sense, so I bring it up. I remind them of Jessica's clowns walking to their gravestones and a mountain inviting her "to join him trembling in the dark." And Julia's ear cartilage made of sprouting African jungles. "If you let words have their way with you, maybe under the influence of music, or of strong feelings or memories, or even under the influence of reading other people's poems (like "anyone lived in a pretty how town"), you may discover things you didn't know you knew. Like how clowns can seem both funny and sad, or that a mountain at night can stir your feelings in a strange way and can seem human—can become a 'he'—or that music can seem to come alive in the ways it enters and spreads through your body. When you write poetry, you may find yourself making a different kind of sense. And often it will be the sense that is made through metaphors—through leading your listeners to connect to things that they normally wouldn't, to visualize, for instance, the mind of a gay man as a room furnished with derogatory names."

Family Sayings: Writing a Second Poem

In establishing some ways in which poetry is different from prose, I don't want the students to conclude that the two have nothing in common—that a story or essay won't benefit from an effective metaphor, that patterns of sound are irrelevant to prose, or that, conversely, a poem can't portray a chain of actions or develop a character. I don't want my journalists, my storytellers, and my lyric poets to stake out one territory and hunker down. Looking ahead to the free-choice project, I decide that we all could benefit from writing a poem that grows from a personal experience, just as we've drawn on "real life" for our profiles, "in the zone" descriptions, the story in Holden's voice, and our writing about a belief we'd stand up for. Even the great poems of fantasy such as Poe's, Coleridge's, and the dream-work of the Surrealists draw inspiration from their authors' feelings—from recognizably human fears, griefs, and dreams. While some of my students will certainly choose to write stories or poems that spring from fantasy, I want them also to discover their own inner journeying. Perhaps they'll discover how personal experience can give color and power to even their wildest inventions. I also want the students to create poems that work with structure, but a structure they could use in a variety of genres, not involving meter or rhyme—no sonnets or villanelles. So I search for a poem we can read together as inspiration for a writing assignment that meets these goals. And I choose Naomi Shihab Nye's poem "Blood."

This moving poem, like "Charlie Howard's Descent" and most of our other reading in the course, explores an aspect of personal identity—in this case, the "blood" that Nye inherited from her Palestinian father. It repeats variants on the refrain "a true Arab," a phrase her father used during Nye's childhood, and it moves chronologically through her life until as an adult she confronts the front-page headlines on a typical day of violence in the Middle East—headlines that "clot" in her blood as she wonders, "Where can the crying heart graze? / What does a true Arab do now?" Like Fugard's play, *"Master Harold,"* the poem implicitly makes the case that the personal is also the political. My students don't have to know much about the Middle East to grasp the poem, but those who have been brought up to sympathize with the Israelis or who have, like many Americans after 9/11, come to view all Arabs as terrorists, will need to open themselves to Nye's emotional truth and let the poem's language "have its way with them."

Therefore, to help prepare students to connect with the poem, I start by asking whether anyone can recall any family sayings, perhaps ones that have become irritants from overuse or ones for which they feel some pride or affection. Jordan tells us that when his mom is mad at him or doesn't want to let him do something he wants to do, she'll say, "Don't you look at me in that tone of voice"—even though he hasn't *said* anything yet. Ayana recalls, "Whenever my big sister and I get into a fight, or she hurts my feelings, my parents will tell me, "'Your sister's all you got.'" Jen mentions how her mom has always said "Sweet dreams" to her at bedtime, "but now I'm grown up she sometimes texts it to me." Matt tells us that whenever he's nervous or scared to take a risk, especially in sports, his dad says, "Just do it." Julia tries to explain, through her giggles, how she and her mom still sing the Almond Joy jingle back and forth to cheer each other up. I tell them how when I was growing up, if any of us five kids complained about anything—and I mean *any*thing—my father would remind us, "Suffering builds character." He made it sound as though character was the be-all and end-all—worth everything. Nonnegotiable. He never discussed what it was.

My brothers and I would groan in unison. As we grew up, it became a sort of dark family joke among us, a line to quote to one another in response to any kind of crisis, great or small.

"Do you think these are things you'll say to your own kids?" I ask them. "Have you internalized them so they're part of you, part of what you remember when you think 'family'? You might also think about family *stories* that get told regularly on particular occasions, with certain turns of phrase that are always the same. Let's brainstorm for a few minutes in our notebooks and see what lines you can remember that are part of the way you've been brought up."

After more sharing, we discover that some families' sayings and stories have to do with taking pride in, or defending, their heritage. Jordan mentions his family's stories about standing up to racial discrimination and participating in the Civil Rights Movement. Ayana says her father tells her of his experiences with discrimination. Jess cites her family's sayings in Italian and Spanish that show pride in both their Italian and their Cuban heritage. Then I hand out copies of "Blood," again with all but the first stanza folded down, and we take turns reading aloud, as we did with "Charlie Howard's Descent," pausing to hear one another's comments and questions. We notice that each time the phrase "true Arab" returns, we learn something new about Nye's heritage and we see her at a different stage in her life. A true Arab "knows how to catch a fly in his hands"; true Arabs "believed watermelon could heal fifty ways"; and Naomi's question when she learns that her father's name, Shihab, means shooting star—"a good name, borrowed from the sky"—is precisely, her father tells her, "what a true Arab would say": "When we die, we give it back?"

Three of the five stanzas begin with an indication of time: "In the spring our palms peeled like snakes," "Years before, a girl knocked," and "Today the headlines clot in my blood." The last stanza stays with "today" but also looks ahead to ask, "What does a true Arab do now?" The opening lines of the third stanza seem to be the most striking for many students:

> *Years before, a girl knocked,*
> *Wanted to see the Arab.*
> *I said we didn't have one.*
> *After that, my father told me who he was,*
> *"Shihab"—"shooting star. . . ."*

I ask the students how they picture this scene, and Nick says he sees Naomi as a little girl, maybe five or six, too little to know that she's part Arab, opening the door and wondering who this other little girl is. He imagines the other girl having maybe been told "*That's* the house where the *Arab* lives." Nick wonders if this happened after 9/11. I explain that the book in which this poem was published, *Words under the Words*, was published in 1980. "Wow, way back then?" he exclaims. Julia, who wrote about anti-Semitism as the thing she'd "stand up against," says that the lines she likes best are about the picture in the headlines—of the little Palestinian who dangles a truck, whom Nye describes as a "homeless fig." She says it's such a touching image, the child so small and helpless like fruit off a tree, and even though she's proud to be Jewish this poem makes her so sad. "I like how Naomi doesn't seem to take sides," Julia says. "It's like she says, and it's true for everybody—the tragedy 'with a terrible root / is too big for us.'"

"Do you see how she's structured the poem around her father's repeated explanations to his daughter about 'what a true Arab is,' and how she moves the poem through different stages of her life as she grows up—into that final question that moves beyond those stages to look into the future?" I ask them. "I think you could do that, and my guess is that you'd find yourself having some interesting memories, maybe making some discoveries, too, about yourself and about writing poetry. Your poem doesn't have to be political, in the way that hers is, though it might end up looking at an issue involving power within a family—and power can be an aspect of the political. Take a look at this sheet with me [see Figure 5.1 on p. 148], and see if you have questions."

I give the students two days to work on their poems and ask them to turn in at least two drafts, their favorite one stapled on top. The next day I ask them for progress reports, as a means of arriving together at some assessment criteria. Jen loves her "Sweet Dreams" poem because "it's only two words but it was such a big part of my childhood. It has such a big impact on me. But I'm having trouble with the line breaks." Jordan says he likes how "vocal and exciting" his poem is. He wasn't sure what he'd write until he got home and heard his mom and sister having a "Don't look at me in that tone of voice" exchange, and then "a whole lot of moments came back, times when she said that to me. I still don't know for sure how I'm going to split it up in stanzas, though." Connor has chosen the word *Goodbye* and is trying to go through a boy's entire life cycle up until his death, but he says it's hard

Draft a poem—shoot for at least 15–20 lines, and start with a freewrite, if you want to—that is, structured around (based on) **repetitions** of a phrase or sentence or question that you've heard repeatedly over the years in your family or extended family, maybe from a parent, or grandparent, or sibling, or other relative. This phrase will be repeated in your poem, maybe in each stanza, and maybe in variant forms, as the spine or frame of the poem, marking different points in your life. (Note how Nye varies her phrase: "A true Arab knows . . . ," "A true Arab believes . . . ," "That's what a true Arab would say," "What does a true Arab do now?"

The second requirement, besides this refrain, is that the poem **must be in stanzas** (though they can be any number and of different lengths). Listen and watch for what the poem "wants," **what shaping and spacing will best serve its ideas and feelings, its images and rhythms.** Where might you need some silence, some pauses? Where can skipping a line for a new stanza help signal this silence?

And third, different parts of the **poem must occur at different times in the speaker's life, signaled by some time indicators where needed** for clarity. See Nye's indicators: "My father **would** say" (shows action continuing over time); "In the spring"; "Years before"; "After that"; "Once"; "Today"; and "Now."

FIGURE 5.1. BORROWING FROM NYE'S POEM "BLOOD."

because "I haven't gone through many of these things, so I have to imagine and still make it realistic." And Ayana, who says she thinks "Blood" may be one of her "favorite poems ever," tells us that using stanzas gave her the idea to make each stanza a grouping of different negatives about her relationship with her sister but end each with a positive, and then break for the refrain, "Your sister's all you got." The class seems eager to hear these poems, so tomorrow we'll have a reading.

"What criteria might be helpful, do you think, not just for assessing tomorrow's draft but to use when you work on it tonight?" I ask them. "Recall what people have been saying about their present drafts, and also what you think made the three poems we've read together memorable—'Charlie Howard's Descent,' 'anyone lived in a pretty how town,' and 'Blood.'" Gradually, as I help the students clarify and combine their ideas, we get a short list on the board. I try not to burden them with a lot of technical language; some kids, I know, are still a little vague about *image* and *metaphor*, and they're feeling their way into what makes effective line and stanza breaks. However, I want them to discover for themselves that poems, like any kind of writing, can be assessed, revised, reassessed, though as with stories, journalism, plays, argument—or music, dance, or painting, for that matter—there's a certain amount of subjectivity involved in the process. "One of my best poetry teachers says that each reader or writer has a different threshold or tolerance for disorder and for order," I tell them. For tonight's poem, based on these students' recent experience with poetry, we arrive at the criteria in Figure 5.2.

Next day, because I sense their interest in hearing one another's poems, I set up a lectern in front of the room and explain that it's easier to enjoy a poetry reading when readers have given some thought to pacing, eye contact, and volume. When readers make us feel that they really want us to enjoy their poems, they've usually done some planning on how to bring this thing on the page to life. I model, reading one of my own poems aloud at the lectern. Then I put students in groups of three to practice, with a checklist for the groups to use in giving each other feedback. Finally, each person goes up to the lectern to read. Before we start, I mention that when I read a new poem of mine to an audience, I sometimes hear words, line breaks, even punctuation that I realize I want to change. So when they go back to their seats, some of them may want to cross out and write in changes.

Connor, who focused his poem on the word *Goodbye*, has helped us imagine how that word might register in a person's throat: as the young

---

Overall, a memorable poem that holds our attention

Good images and metaphors that make us feel and think

Line breaks and stanza breaks that serve the poem

Words and word combinations that make clear pictures

Good use of sounds, especially of the refrain

Punctuation and caps (or lowercase) that serve the poem

All three requirements from the direction sheet present

FIGURE 5.2. *CRITERIA FOR ASSESSING AND REVISING A POEM.*

boy says goodbye over his great-grandmother's coffin, "he finds it difficult to form the horrible / word in his throat, / the word that will put a lock on her coffin and send her / away on the salty ocean breeze." In another stanza, the boy's father sends him off to college: "Even his father, calm and reserved, can barely utter / the pointed phrase." At the end, the boy, now a dying old man, feels "the last guttural word / lodged in his throat" as he says goodbye to his wife. In each stanza, Connor has used an image of water—the ocean in the first three and a tear in the last. I ask the class whether they are hearing this poem primarily as a story, as episodes in a man's life, and Jess says, "Well, sort of, but it's different from a story. It's more about feelings, and it's cool how he used the ocean for almost every key moment. It kind of makes you feel change, like waves. And it—uh—it makes you see how change is always there, like the ocean."

Julia has used the Almond Joy jingle she'd told us about earlier: "Sometimes you feel like a nut, sometimes you don't. Almond Joy's got nuts! Mounds don't." Her poem is fun to listen to, partly because she's brave enough to sing the lines each time they appear. In one stanza, "our jingle" turns up in a muggy summer in the city, plastered against the Hershey Factory: " . . . Right there, / on cue in the middle of the Big Apple, I began / singing, moving my arms and hips to that unusual beat, *Sometimes you feel like a nut*. . . ." The poem ends at Julia's bat mitzvah, where her mother's speech concludes with a smile and

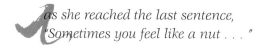

> *as she reached the last sentence,*
> *"Sometimes you feel like a nut . . . "*
>
> *We were the only ones who got it.*
> *We were the only nuts.*

As we finish hearing the poems, I ask, "Are there any of you who might want to write more poems?" Almost every hand goes up.

So Far/What Next?

Through this combination of reading and writing poems—approximately a week and a half's worth of class time and homework, including the day for our visiting artist—most of the students seem to have developed a new openness toward poetry. They've rediscovered the fun of wordplay, of unfolding stories, of nonsense and beyond-sense, that many remember experiencing in their elementary school exposure to poems. But they've also started to think about ways in which writing poetry is related to writing various kinds of prose. They've seen Mark Doty unfold a story that is both suspenseful and reflective, that shifts pace and point of view, that through image and metaphor can both stir our feelings and challenge our assumptions. They've realized from their work with E. E. Cummings's poem of strange syntax, puzzling images, and haunting refrains; from their own automatic or stream of consciousness writing to music; and from their reliance on seemingly random word combinations, that fresh language isn't necessarily accessed through logic and dictionaries. They've learned that the personal can be political—that a poem like Nye's "Blood" can draw inspiration from memories of family and from current headlines and photos in the newspaper. And they've found that the process of creating a poem may invite them to challenge the conventions of English usage, if doing so "makes the poem better."

As the students move toward their free-choice project, for which I plan to allot the next three weeks, they should be able to look back over a variety of genres they've explored both as readers and as writers to consider which one they most enjoyed—or perhaps, if they already have material in mind that they want to write about, which genre is best suited to that material. So I ask them to think about this project tonight and jot down some ideas in their notebooks.

Next day I ask hopefully, "So last night did any of you discover that as a writer you're finding out you have a favorite genre? Or maybe that you're starting to know what kind of material you want to write about for the free-choice project?" Gradually, about two-thirds of the hands go up. I call on Peter, who's looking eager. Peter says he thinks he knows what he wants to write but he's not sure there's a name for it. It's going to be funny like Mark Twain and have some Greek gods in it and maybe a sort of utopia with this huge disaster—like a, what's it called, uh, a big *apocalypse*—at the end.

Garret gives a long whistle, which I guess means "Deep!" And I suggest we may have a new genre here.

Chapter 6

The Free-Choice Project: "I want to write something I'd enjoy reading"

*D*ear Ms. Michaels, for my creative writing piece I've chosen to write a series of letters which will create a story and relationship. I've narrowed my choices down to:

(1) A series of letters between family members, such as two cousins. I would model these on my relationship with my own cousin (we are both 14 and girls but we live in different countries). Since we have some key similar personality traits, I'd play with the levels of intensity and spice up the characters so there is a mix of reality and fiction. The letters would be about friendships, families, memories, boys, school, etc. It would become an insight into a close bond but also in the lives of two teens in two countries. I haven't yet figured how to work each of our tales together to create a point, but I can brainstorm.

(2) Or I could write about two childhood friends, a boy and a girl in their early twenties, whose relationship and courtship grows through their letters. I'm thinking of the 1920's and 30's as a time period. Possibly the boy has gone to find employment and the girl's letters are reminiscing about their shared memories as children. Maybe they made a secret pact when they were younger to live in a fantasy somewhere together, and that hope is being torn by the distance between them.

*D*ear Julia: Creating characters and relationships through letters could be a lot of fun! The question of what *conflict* can arise between your two letter writers for you to explore seems like an interesting challenge In the first proposal. You say "point," but the point (or significance or meanings—the "why does this matter to us?") will probably arise out of conflicts that arise between the characters and their worlds, as you explore them. Whereas in your second proposal, you already have rich possibilities for conflict: within your setting—the Depression—and in courtship at a distance (lots of room for misunderstandings, economic pressures, family feelings, childhood fantasies vs. adult practicalities. Lots of potential for *character development, too*). Would you need to do *research* if you went with choice #2? I think you studied the Depression in history last year, right? Whichever you choose, discovering *why the relationship matters* could be fun for you.

Initial email exchange between Julia and me

Ms. Michaels, here's my proposal. Sorry it's so late, I got home from basketball really late. I think I'm going to change the main character's name, though.

> 16 year old Leonardo Diamond has never had a normal life, not after the house fire that killed his parents and sister 3 years ago. He is the only one that knows the truth: The fire was not accidental and was actually set by the U.S. government to keep his family from telling a secret that, if out, would break down the dictatorship of America. But America is now the colony of Kronos, named after its dictator. L. must set out on his quest of revenge for his dead family, his hunt to find and kill Kronos. Along the way he meets a few Kronians who are all as against the dictatorship as he is. But there are many loyal subjects and the going is rough. People are lost along the way. L. is struggling on the outside to fight the evil that is overthrowing free America, but also on the inside to let go of the grief, anger, and pain that has built up over the years.

Dear Jenna: It's great that you're thinking about both a broad, public conflict *and* one individual's internal conflict. But the outline sounds like a humongous novel to me! And you have only a couple of weeks to write it. Even if you don't show us the fire episode, you'd have to create enough sense of L's family and his relationship with them to make his "grief, anger, and pain" real to us. Then there's the broad picture of a whole country, and creating enough adventures on the quest so as to show the anti-dictator Kronians in action and some of those "getting lost along the way" (more episodes?) plus the stuff that the many loyal subjects do against the hero. And you'll need to paint a convincing picture of "the evil that's overthrowing free America." You can't just tell us all this; to bring it to life, you'll have to *show* it, illustrate it. Create whole scenes, linked by summaries. And there's the 8-page limit.

Maybe if you're wedded to the idea of a revenge quest, you could write just one "chapter," one adventure, starting with a flashback in his mind to the fire and little memories, just flashes, of moments with a family member, as he's engaging with some loyal and some rebellious Kronians? Before you go any further, **I'd like you to email me tonight** how Leonardo's situation and his anti-dictator quest came to you—various memories of stories or movies and personal imaginings that gave you inspiration—and what aspects made it feel like it would be fun to write about. **I can be more helpful if I know this.**

Initial email exchange between Jenna and me:

The Project

Julia's and Jenna's proposals are first drafts, written in response to the directions in Figure 6.1 after some discussion and some work with a "preview" form in class.

Commentary

Notice how much I've emphasized to the students that they shouldn't feel locked into their initial ideas and should look forward to making discoveries in every aspect of their piece as they work on it. Like Ralph Fletcher and many other writer-teachers, I know from my own experience as a poet to be "leery of prewriting exercises" (132). Some of the students will change their proposals overnight, after the first email. I definitely want them to have room for trial and error, for spontaneous discoveries of their own, but I don't want them to write for ten days and then ask to start over with a totally new idea. We don't have that kind of time. While I greet each proposal with as much enthusiasm and encouragement as I honestly can, I also want to spot problems that are likely to prove insoluble. The class has agreed to take responsibility for pursuing the implications of their choices, but as a more experienced writer I can point out a few of those implications for them. From watching me do this they can start to learn how to do it for themselves. Certainly they need to experience the thrill of taking some risks—especially the thrill of discovering new possibilities as they write. It is a delicate balancing

1. Please email me tonight by 8:30 PM a proposal for your writing project. This proposal should describe your project, as far as you can predict just now. You'll make new discoveries as you write, over the next two weeks; the proposal is just a preliminary sketch, so don't feel locked into it. Adjust my questions as necessary to fit your ideas but do try to address the following in your description:

    a. What question or conflict or tension (external? internal?) might make the situation, character(s), or speaker/narrator/inter- viewee interesting to you—and, potentially, to us? If this is a fictitious or partly fictional person or situation, what do you "know" (imaginatively) about her, him, or it so far? This imag- ining will develop further, maybe in surprising ways, as you write during these next 2 weeks.

    b. If time(s) and/or place(s) seem important to the piece, de- scribe what you know about them so far and how you imagine they might be significant. Again, significance may develop as your piece develops, in ways you can't foresee right now.

    c. If you plan to interview one or more people, when and how will you contact them and set up times to talk? Specify at least ten questions you'd like to ask one or more of them and a "lens" through which you plan to focus the interview, though that lens may change as you find out more about them, and new questions will certainly arise.

2. Now start writing your piece, and write for a good 30 minutes at least, just to start getting acquainted with some possibilities. (If it's to be based on interviews, you might start with a description or imagi- nary scene to get us interested in this person or help us feel your interest.) SAVE a copy of this writing to work with in class tomorrow on the laptop or in your notebook and to show me.

FIGURE 6.1. DIRECTIONS FOR THE PROJECT PROPOSAL.

act. Julia, for example, turns out to be happy to pursue her second choice, after thinking over my questions, and seems proud to be able to draw on her own knowledge of the Depression as well as invent her courting couple pretty much from scratch rather than basing characters on herself and her cousin. Jenna, on the other hand, in response to my cautioning, moves at once to an entirely different kind of story, about a runaway from an orphanage, begging on the New York City streets to pay for a plane ticket to California to look for the parents who'd seemingly abandoned her. A young man who gives her money on the street will prove to be her brother and unknowingly reunite her with their parents. Jen would later write, in answer to my wrap-up questions about the projects, that she realized from my first reactions that her initial story would be "way too long," and so she came up with her second plot, though originally with the man being a lover, not the brother. "But I wouldn't have had enough pages for them to have fallen in love, and the brother/sister [relationship] worked out better anyway." I think my concerns about her initial proposal showed her the need to consider how much detail it takes to make a relationship's development seem real. She explained that her inspiration for this new story came mostly from her imagination but also from "romantic type movies." Then "toward the end I added a twist in the plot that even I didn't know about." Jenna was learning from her project how planning and spontaneity can operate together in the creative process. In her final comment, however, I could hear some frustration along with the pride: "I liked the descriptions and suspense in my final story, but I could have made it better and done what I really wanted to do if it could have been longer."

Drafting the Proposals

As we share their first notebook jottings about project choices (see Chapter 5) and begin to plan the proposals that students will email me, the most vociferous questioners want to know about length. I ask for their suggestions. It's difficult to set a length limit given the range of possible genres and the varying levels of concentration and writing fluency among the kids, but after brief discussion, and to protect myself, I tell them I can't make time to read anything longer than eight pages, especially if I read several drafts. I set four pages as the minimum, thinking in particular of the two students who say they might want to write a group of poems; my experience with young teen poetry is that shorter is generally better, and that effective cutting and restructuring often takes much longer than the poets anticipate.

But the more important and much more interesting issue, for us and for any class and teacher who undertake this kind of project, is that of originality. My teenage writers are immersed in a world with which I have minimal familiarity, despite my best resolutions—a world of horror/romance movies,

video game adventures, sci fi, rock videos, MTV, Facebook, fashion magazines, YouTube posts, and a huge range of websites. All of this is a valid part
of their personal experience and a background they share with one another,
at least to some extent—a world that shapes their imaginations and that
they can reference, just as in my writing I draw from jazz and classical music; poetry; New York theater, dance, and art; my favorite *New York Times*
columnists (Gail Collins, yes!); and my own coming of age in the 1960s.
How can I best help them "steal" rather than "borrow," as T. S. Eliot put it?
To me, *borrow* in Eliot's locution (talent borrows, genius steals) basically
means to plagiarize—to appropriate without the imaginative transformation that happens naturally with a good writer on both the conscious and
subconscious levels. "Borrowing" can be a sometimes mindless, sometimes
all too crafty, cut-and-paste operation, the insertion of five lines of Internet
poetry into one's own poem without attribution or any stated purpose of collage, or the simple retelling of a movie plot as one's own. Taking someone
else's idea, unchanged, implies you could then return it to them, exactly as
it was, no problem! But when Jess later writes me that she knows that one
of her heroine's nightmares, in which she sees herself killing a friend on the
school playground, was influenced by a scene from the movie based on J.
K. Rowling's *The Prisoner of Azkaban* ("where they do such a good job on the
effects of making everything seem so dark and mysterious, from the setting
to the saturation of the film, to the music—it's all so real"), I know, rereading her character's nightmare, that Jess has transformed this memory of the
movie scene by setting hers in a playground, with its terrifyingly familiar
childhood associations, and that in doing this she has made it truly her own.
She has "stolen" rather than "borrowed." I feel very little surprise when she
goes on to tell me that the three nightmares in her story are drawn from
her own personal experience—"I don't want to scare you, but I actually had
these quite frequently last year, especially [in] the weeks right after the
deaths of people close to me."

　　To help my students think about the sometimes highly puzzling question
of where their ideas and images are coming from, and to give them permission to blend "real" with imaginary (as well as to give myself some help in
steering them away from borrowing, toward stealing), I ask them to fill out
in class the form in Figure 6.2. It also offers another chance to emphasize
the reading–writing connection. (I geared the first question more toward fictional narrative, since so many of the students say they're planning to write
fiction.)

1. If you were to create a character somewhat based on yourself, mixing the real and the imaginary, *what changes might you make in yourself* and what personality traits, past experiences, interests, values, family background, and other background elements *might you keep the same?* (Recall how Hally and Holden were partly inspired by their authors' real experiences.)

2. Think over the pieces you've written this fall but also imagine one you'd like to write. Consider: Which of the following aspects of writing do you enjoy doing most? Circle as many as you wish:

    a. dialogue

    b. monologue

    c. descriptions of people, places, states of mind

    d. narrating action sequences

    e. exploring imagery

    f. creating rhythms, rhymes, other sound patterns

    g. interviewing people for profile

    h. narrating/reflecting on personal experience

    i. creating an imaginary (fantasy? sci fi?) world or society

    j. exploring feelings and/or relationships

    k. writing poetry (to music? out of personal experience? imagined experience?)

    l. satirizing, making fun of something, parodying

3. What subjects/situations/kinds of people or places interest you—and why?

4. Based on what a student said last year at this time—"I want to write something that I'd enjoy reading"—what kinds of reading do you most enjoy?

5. If by now you have some sense of the kind of writing you'd most enjoy working on for this project, describe that briefly here, as a start on the proposal you'll send me tonight.

FIGURE 6.2. REFLECTING, REMEMBERING, AND BRAINSTORMING TOWARD THE PROJECT.

By the next day, I've received and responded to everyone's proposals. To at least half the class I found myself writing at least one of the following questions:

> What interests you most in your project so far—what are you most looking forward to?
>
> Do you believe you can bring to life for us—in two weeks—this much action, character change, passage of time?
>
> Where do you see potential for conflict, tension?
>
> In what aspects of the story/character/subject/issues/feelings might you be able to draw on your own experience (which could mean your emotional experience—of, say, panic, jealousy, love)?
>
> Will you enjoy exploring your project for two solid weeks?
>
> What influences or sources do you think may be inspiring your idea?

I admit, I was up pretty late last night. But I discovered with last year's projects that the initial emailing and second-guessing pays off. Just a caution: don't schedule these projects with more than one class at a time. Stagger them. It's mind-draining enough to troubleshoot proposals for just one class, let alone keep track of each student's progress over two or three weeks of steady in-school and out-of-school writing—more difficult, I think, than working with research papers, because one is constantly shifting gears from genre to genre and dealing with the unpredictable workings of the imagination.

Pacing these next two weeks is tricky. I've promised to give no other homework and to devote each day's class to the project (aside from the usual five minutes or so of free reading). But I remind everyone that under "project" belong mini-lessons on various aspects of writing, additional interviewing for the profiles, appointments with a Writing Center mentor, breaks for impromptu peer responses whenever two people choose to ask each other for feedback, library research, conferences with me. . . . I know it's important that my writers feel they have enough time to write a lot—to stash in a separate folder on their desktop entire pages that don't seem to be working. But some of them will go nuts if they think they have to write for fifty minutes of class day after day.

Making the Rounds

By the time I've approved all the proposals, nearly everyone is clicking away on the laptops, except for Sydney, who's writing a poem in her notebook. I cruise the room with my clipboard and copies of the proposals. Connor is in a corner, fully absorbed in his partially autobiographical tale of two cousins tracking animals together in South Africa. Highly athletic and competitive like their parents and both in their early twenties, Hannah is looking for adventure and excitement while Colin, the narrator, "who is often teased about being so short" (yes, Connor's the shortest in his grade), wants adventure "but also calm and joy." They have just returned to their camp to find it torn apart—"I would bet it was a warthog." Eventually, Connor's characters will find "more excitement than they wanted." Jess and Jenna are typing fast and each gives me that annoyed, preoccupied glance of a writer in the throes of creation. Ayana, Jessica, and James have all left for the library to do some research as a preliminary to interviewing various family members—Ayana on the subject of what Obama's election means to different generations of African Americans, including her own; Jessica on her father's career as a pediatrician and her own thoughts about becoming a doctor; and James on his grandfather's role as a clinical psychologist who in 1961 helped NASA evaluate test pilots as potential astronauts. When I reach Hunt, he's staring dreamily into space, an empty screen in front of him.

"Hunt, how did it go last night, the writing? Could you show me?" It turns out he had two big tests to study for last night. But, politely, he opens the document and shows me his four lines. The protagonist, a boy who seems to be a combination of Hunt and Holden Caulfield, has so far succeeded, groggily, in turning off his alarm clock. My heart sinks. Sustained effort is just not easy for this bright, interesting kid. Hunt's proposal begins:

> I will do my piece about the average day in the life of a teenager around my age. I will make him a spacey kid, whose mind often wanders when he is in classes or becomes uninterested in what is going on. I will write everything that goes through his head. He can go to school, hang out with friends, go to a party. I will write from his point of view. He will go through conflicts with teachers, and internal arguments convincing himself to go talk to a girl he has a crush on, going out onto the dance floor at the party, etc.

I'm wondering how Hunt feels about this kid. I consider reminding him of the complex and shifting reactions the class had to Holden: how they wanted to figure out what makes him the way he is and whether he's likely to change; how they discussed what keeps us interested in his point of view. Should I suggest that Hunt just freewrite a bit to explore his own thoughts and feelings about the character he's creating? No, maybe that would hit too close to home or make him too self-conscious. I'm also worried by that "everything" in his proposal. This story could end up as what Ralph Fletcher calls "the much maligned 'bed-to-bed' story [that] results from the writer's inability to exclude any moment, no matter how trivial, from a particular day" (124). But right now Hunt probably just needs to get his narrator out of bed and out the front door—not look ahead and worry. He needs to redis-cover what it feels like to be writing. "Hunt," I urge, "just read over those four lines to get back into this boy's thoughts and voice—read them aloud, under your breath, and listen for what he'll say and do next. Type whatever you hear. Just drift along with him on the page, and when I come back in ten minutes, I want to see him up and out of the house, encountering some-thing or someone at school. I'm really curious to hear what his mind sounds like, and where he goes in his mind." Hunt nods, and behind my back I cross my fingers.

I move on to Sydney, who's working on a poem about her grandmother, a part Native American, part Caribbean woman whom she loves deeply. Sydney has proposed to write a group of poems that will grow out of her strongest emotions, including her anger and hurt and sense of guilt over her parents' divorce, her experience of falling in love, and maybe her urge to write poetry. I noticed how naturally she gravitated to imagery in writing her "in the zone" piece, especially images rooted in the body—tension and release, heaviness and lightness. In responding to her proposal, I suggested that such visceral images could serve her well. Sydney shows me her note-book: "I know I want to describe the turquoise pendant my grandmother always wears, but I don't know how to get into it. I've just got a list of words here. I don't want it to get cheesy and sentimental."

Or clichéd. I've found that working within a form has often helped me deal with these problems in my own poems, but I don't want to give Syd-ney a mini-lesson on sonnets or sestinas. Suddenly I remember a prompt I often use in the spring poetry unit, and I root around in the bookcase till I find my William Carlos Williams. I show her "The Red Wheelbarrow," read it aloud, and suggest that she begin her draft with "So much depends / upon . . ." Not only will this focus her on the necklace right away and encourage her to linger on the image for a while without any of the abstract nouns and clichés of sentiment, but also it invites the visceral image of weight, the physical sense of *depend*—"hang down from," which is what a heavy stone pendant does. At the same time, the literal image enables Sydney to play with the double meaning of *depend*, if she wants to, and could move her from the literal to the figurative. Gradually the poem may unfold—to the writer and her readers—the mysteries of what the "so much" might be.

"Try stealing his first line and a half, and just keep writing to see where they lead you. Williams's line and stanza breaks may free you up, too, if you get them into your ear and eye. They may make your voice more conversational, help you listen for moments where silence and white space and breathing can help convey your feelings. 'No ideas but in things,' he said. The turquoise is a thing that may help you explore the idea of your feelings for your grandmother. You can always cut off those two first lines later if you want to; just let them get you started. Or if you keep them, you could reference Williams right under your own title—*after Williams Carlos Williams*—though sometimes these days if the source is very recognizable, writers don't include the reference." Sydney looks interested. A few days later, she brings me her latest draft:

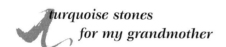
turquoise stones
for my grandmother

so much depends
upon those

sleek turquoise stones

pressed in the

ancient tarnished silver

strung around that

slender terracotta neck
as it turns
head shaking from

old memories
and how they're still fresh
the necklace a part of her
soon to be bequeathed

to her other gems.

Sydney says she'd forgotten how her grandmother calls her and her sister "my gems" until she'd gotten a good way through the draft. "And then, wow! It made just the right ending." I ask her to read her poem to the class and talk about her process, especially to try to explain how her ending "happened." "It's important to realize that sometimes you can just trust the words and feelings that are operating together as you write," I tell everyone. "Or that as a character or voice becomes more and more fully defined, you can trust it to 'know' what to say and do. Or sometimes if your writing evokes a place powerfully enough, your instincts will know what should happen next in that place. I'm guessing that Connor's Africa—both his memories of the actual place and his imagining of it in his story—will help him discover sooner or later how his story 'needs' to end. Maybe the same thing with the nightmares Jess is describing in her psychological thriller. You did some of the initial planning in your proposal, and you may have developed these plans further by now, but *stay flexible.* Allow the writing to 'tell you' what it wants, as you read it aloud and listen to it appearing on the page. And in particular, don't get wedded to a specific ending. If you keep revisiting your piece, it will often show you an ending that grows naturally from the story or poem or profile. It could still be a surprise or 'twist' ending, but it won't seem contrived, artificial, imposed from outside the story. It may shed new light on the piece's events and characters, it may leave us thinking about human nature, relationships, values—but if it has flowed naturally from the rest of the piece, then it won't sound like a tacked-on moral."

Mini-Lessons

Since I have only two students writing poetry, I can give them quick conferences in class as the need arises. But for the narratives, whether fictional or
based on interviews, questions of structure and pace are soon arising daily.
Hands wave at me frantically. Though I have almost no experience writing
fiction, I'm comfortable narrating scenes of action and dialogue from my
own life in and out of the classroom. Still, after last year's projects, I realized I needed help in creating some useful mini-lessons on narrative, so first
I turned to Janet Burroway's classic college text, *Writing Fiction: A Guide to
Narrative Craft*. Although it's very helpful for older students and for teachers, the examples and language are beyond most fourteen-year-olds. However, between Burroway's sections on narrative time—especially the one on
summary versus scene—and Ralph Fletcher's section, "A Playfulness with
Time" in *What a Writer Needs*, I cobbled together a short lesson and exercise
to help move my writers beyond the primitive linear structure of "Then
. . . . Next" and beyond a uniform texture in which all moments are equally
important.

When Ralph Fletcher came to our school some years ago, I sat in on his
session with the creative writing class, in which he focused on ways to recognize and to crack open the "hot spot" of one's piece (a useful metaphor he
attributes to Karen Howell). Fletcher cautions

> As teachers we cannot presume to know exactly where the hot spot lies in
> students' stories. What may seem important to us may be of little interest
> to the writer, and vice versa. But once the student has identified the hot
> spot, we can suggest ways of slowing the writing. By . . . lingering at the
> crucial moment, the writer helps the reader to discover the relative impor-
> tance of various events and characters in the writing. (133–34)

He suggests that one of the most effective ways of slowing time is to write a
dramatic scene, and then offers very clear examples of both scene and summary. He explains that the dramatic scene is a powerful tool that can do
many things:

> Slow the action, introducing dialogue and gesture
> Make the narrator an active character rather than a passive storyteller

Allow the reader to experience the grief/delight of the story at the same
time the narrator does

Give readers the raw materials of the story so they can infer larger issues
(134)

Fletcher compares this technique to that of a movie director using slow motion to draw out a crucial moment. In addition to discussing his explanation
and examples with my class, I chose examples from *Catcher in the Rye* to
illustrate differences between summary and scene. The first two paragraphs
of the closing chapter in *Catcher* ("I could probably tell you what I did after
I went home, and how I got sick and all, and what school I'm supposed to go
to next fall. . . .") offer a good example of *summary*—covering a lot of time
and events quickly and expeditiously with no details. It's a very effective
use of summary, not simply for creating suspense while wrapping things
up fast but for preserving Holden's characteristic voice and point of view.
The fight with Sally Hayes, from Chapter 17, offers a fine example of *scene;*
Salinger slows the pace way down to let Holden show us through action,
dialogue, and reflection the utterly different values of these two characters.
And then, because student examples are often much more powerful than
literary ones—as Fletcher says, "a strategy does not become part of the 'class
culture' until students see their peers using that strategy" (125)—I ask Matt
to read aloud a brief scene from the basketball story he's writing:

> I could not wait until the first practice. Each minute seemed like an hour,
> and each hour a day. Nothing else could penetrate my mind that day
> except basketball. In high spirits, I strolled into the gym with my head held
> high until I saw Mr. Thomas, the head Varsity coach, approach me with a
> blank look stretched across his whole face.
>
> "You can't practice," he blurted out.
>
> No words came out of my mouth.
>
> "Unless you get an average of C + or higher, you are not permitted to
> step one foot on my basketball court."
>
> He then turned his back and walked toward the rest of the guys. The
> smart guys that were allowed to play basketball because they tried hard to
> get high grades.

My homework assignment for that night (for everyone, regardless of
genre):

> **Write for at least 30 more minutes.** (This writing could include some rewriting, depending on what you feel your piece needs, but keep our time frame in mind.) **Then reread your handout** from Fletcher's chapter about scene vs. summary. **Now review your whole draft**, including the new part, to see whether there is a "hot spot" you might slow down for one or more of the purposes that Fletcher lists. Choose the "hottest spot" you can find, **and rewrite it as a dramatic scene**. SAVE your complete draft, with the new scene included, for class tomorrow.

When final drafts of the projects eventually arrived on my desk, I could see this lesson had borne fruit. The only two students who had not managed to create scenes in their narratives had both gotten off to a very slow start with their projects due to lack of planning and concentration and, in one case, some computer problems. Both were in the habit of turning work in late or not at all. One never got to the Writing Center for a conference. Interestingly, he had decided to write a movie-influenced story about a teenage girl drugged at a party and later kidnapped. His chief interest, he said, was in her very strict parents finally giving in to the girl's pleas to attend this party, which they suspected would have no adult supervision; he pointed the moral very firmly at the end: "This was a lesson for teens and parents, to not give into peer pressure and for parents to trust their first instinct." He was also excited about the story line: "The kidnapper hits her on the head and brings her into the house where an older man locks her up. When she awakes Carly is suffering from memory loss and is convinced the seven people in the house are her family. Throughout this story, Carly tries to fight her flashbacks or what her so called family is saying." This writer spent all his writing time trying to cover—summarize—the numerous events of his plot and to figure out how the girl was to be rescued. He wrote in third person with very little sense of voice and, given the lack of scenes, very little character development. He barely completed a draft on time.

On the other hand, as I read over this kid's wrap-up comments, I can tell that the project was in many ways a satisfying experience for him:

> My favorite part was when Carly's parents gave in and leading up to the party. I enjoyed writing about this because it's something that parents and kids in real life go through. I liked having this realistic storyline to lead up to the kidnapping. I liked getting to read part of it aloud and hear other people read theirs. It made it feel like we were all on the same level.

And, despite earning a C+ on the piece, he said he'd learned more about writing:

> Ms. M. and the peer editing helped me open up more on information that seemed hidden in the story. My weaknesses are fading off in places and having too little dialogue. . . . I have to know when to go more in depth of a specific part and when to pull away and be less specific. Doing the project will help me be more animated and expressive with papers in general.

And finally, I think simply having two weeks in which to create a story was exciting for a student who, at his previous school, had been told to write an entire story over the weekend.

Visits to the Writing Center

I find myself giving more mini-lessons as the need arises, introducing new information and sometimes reviewing earlier work that the students suddenly find relevant: on punctuating dialogue; on ways to indicate shifts in time and place; on streamlining dialogue; on the different "sounds" of the dash, the semicolon, and the colon; on ways to balance one's own voice with that of the person one is interviewing; on useful questions to bring to the writing mentors. As I make my rounds in class each day, I try to help each student figure out when a visit to the Writing Center would be most useful.

Some of the mentors email me whenever they've had a conference with one of my students, but if they forget to do this, I go to the center and skim the forms they've filled out on each conference. Figure 6.3 documents the key information from Lindsay's filed form on her conference with James. James took his own notes on the draft he read aloud to Lindsay. I require students to include with the draft they submit to me any drafts they read to a writing mentor or a peer responder, along with the relevant notes and forms and a comment about what was or was not helpful in these sessions. With the free-choice project, I also collected a wrap-up questionnaire, a kind of exit interview, which gave me a lot more information than I normally get about a single piece of writing. From this form, it's clear that James found Lindsay's advice very useful. But I think, too, the advice about incorporating his own feelings was more acceptable coming from her, a respected older student writer, than from me, an aging female teacher-poet. James is at heart a journalist, a little suspicious of blurring the crisp facts of a "report" with emotion. However, he writes: "I received a lot of great advice from the Writing Mentor. I learned a lot about my grandfather from this project, but I also learned that adding personal reflections to a piece can make it a lot more interesting. I will most definitely use this technique in future pieces."

In every instance but one, students are coming back to class full of praise for the mentors, and by the end of the project, all but one student has chosen to have at least one conference. I'm impressed with the advice given and taken. Nick, with his long story of how a "perfect day" morphs into a "really bad, life-changing day," was jumping around over seventeen years in the life of his twelfth-grade character; Rebecca praises his "deep internal examination" of the narrator and several "nice insights" but focuses on how to keep the story moving along, clarify some "murky sections," and separate more clearly the past memories from the present day. "Cohesiveness, that's what to work on," she tells him. Julia takes her mentor's advice to work

---

Mentor _____Student _____ Grade_____ Date_____

Course_____ Teacher_____ Advisor_____

Days until assignment is due_____

Did someone refer student to Writing Center?_____

May we share this form with your teacher? _____

Writing issues discussed: Moving beyond chronology, adding emotion and a little bit of himself (James) to his grandfather's story.

What possibilities or specific recommendations grew out of discussion? We decided a second interview was in line, to come up with how Mr. Powell felt in all this, what effects working with the test pilots had on him, and how James is discovering what this story means to him (James).

Follow-up plan: Revise with info from a second interview.

Figure 6.3. Sample Writing Center conference form.

on building more tension between her two characters by having the young woman write her lover one more letter. Garret, writing a semiautobiographical story about a boy getting lost on a camping trip, can't figure out how to incorporate any dialogue into his first-person narrative until his mentor suggests having two boys get lost together. Rebecca suggests to Peter that his conclusion seems pretty abrupt and that a scene showing the final conflict between his Greek gods returning to earth might help. She also recommends smoother transitions between the modern narrator's view and the gods' view. I suspect that her interest gives Peter the motivation he needs to revise an already strong story. Connor, who's worked independently and perhaps a bit complacently, finds that his mentor's praise of his imagery makes it easier to accept the suggestions about condensing repetitive sections and wordiness, along with the quick lesson on *less* versus *fewer*. (I'm impressed that any student cares about, let alone understands, the difference.) Matt, who has introduced into his story an absent dad, at first away on business trips but currently dead, seizes on his mentor's excellent advice to move the story of the dad's death "to a place in the story where it will have greater impact" and also give a few more details about the boy's relationship with his mother. And Brooks, who never bothered to learn from me how to indent and punctuate dialogue, is suddenly making the effort now that his older guy mentor has raised this issue. Also, the story is important to Brooks—"It was great to be able to do *anything* in our story with no limitations"—and he says that Brian "helped me see ways I could make it more realistic." Clearly, Brian's interest in the story's promise increased Brooks's willingness to fuss with punctuation.

Assessment, Peer Response

During the last few days before deadline, we discuss possible criteria to use in revising, peer response, and assessment. Along with the elements they've learned to consider from their previous pieces (titles, incorporation of dialogue, sensory details, openings and closings, etc.), the students add several new ones that have grown from the past two weeks' mini-lessons, impromptu conferences in class and via email, and visits to the Writing Center. We decide to pose the criteria as questions, which we then synthesize into a list (see Figure 6.4).

1. Why is this story or poem or profile being told? Do we care? Does it feel urgent?
2. Is the narrating/writing voice interesting? believable?
3. Is there a good use of dramatic scenes for the hot spot(s)?
4. Is time handled clearly, effectively—time shifts? quick summaries? flashbacks? slowed down for scenes?
5. Are there any unnecessary parts that should be condensed or cut?
6. Believable conflict(s)? Well motivated? Clear what character(s) wants?
7. Good word choice to create sensory details and precise imagery?

FIGURE 6.4. CRITERIA FOR THE FREE-CHOICE PROJECT.

Some students have already done quick responses to one another's project drafts, but even so, all agree they'd like to have a full period to get feedback before final revisions. To the new questions we've arrived at as criteria, along with our previous ones, I add one on setting and the usual cluster of items to circle on formatting. I also ask everyone to recommend an excerpt (maybe three to five minutes long) that their partner should read aloud at our celebration party. Next day I'm struck by how even my most distractible students spend most of our fifty minutes working with their partners. Discussions seem enthusiastic and focused. As I look over shoulders, I can see a lot of good suggestions for what to read aloud.

Celebratory Reading

In preparation for the reading party, I put these same partners together, seated opposite each other on the floor, some in the classroom, some in the hall, and for about twenty minutes they rehearse their excerpts. Each gives feedback to the other on appropriate variations in volume, pace, and eye contact; expressiveness and clarity. "Not just enunciation of individual words, but help us to hear the shifts of speakers, of emotion, of time and place," I tell them. "You've all had to listen to kids read aloud badly, BORINGLY. Who wants to be bored? You've picked strong excerpts. Engage us with them right from the start. Make us feel that you care about keeping us interested, that you *want* us to hear this piece. Eye contact from time to time makes a big difference; remember how we worked with this the first day of school, reading "Eye-to-Eye" aloud, and how Hunt and Nick and Julia demonstrated it for us when we did scenes from *Catcher*? The other thing to decide with your partner is how much you need to tell us before you read, how much *context* we might need in order to understand your excerpt. Your three to five minutes includes any preliminary explanation, so keep it short, and practice it now, with your partner. Oh, and make sure you give us your title—clearly, and with a little pause so we can take it in."

For the reading, I divide the class in half since I know that listening to every student read will take too long. We use our classroom and the Writing Center, which I reserve. We decide on some not-too-messy refreshments. I create new pairs within the two groups; these new partners will each fill out a brief form on the other's reading, a checklist with room for one comment that can be used unobtrusively and quickly (see Figure 6.5).

At Garret's request, we serve cupcakes. I wish I could clone myself and be in both rooms, but I nip back and forth, making sure to catch some

---

Title_____ Author_____

\+ (outstanding)   * (area needs work)   – (weakness distracting)

Appropriate variation in:

      ___volume

      ___pace

      ___emphasis

      ___eye contact

Clarity in:

      ___enunciation

      ___context

      ___shifts in speakers, time, place, tone

Comment:_____

FIGURE 6.5. *ASSESSMENT OF PROJECT PRESENTATIONS.*

part of each reading. As I think back now, more than a year later, and flip through my copies of the students' projects, I can see the individual faces—one peering up bravely at us from under long bangs, another through dark glasses, a third grinning, mouth stained with chocolate cake—and I can hear the voices. Jessica reads from her opening, her dad's description of the ICU:

> At 11:00 at night, the ICU is scary. You enter through two big metal doors and come up through a nursing station, which is basically a big long desk with monitors. On either side are two open areas, each with four beds. There is very little privacy. There are patients in all the other spots. There are nurses and therapists scurrying about, all speaking in hushed tones. A constant beeping of monitors. It is noisy and quiet at the same time. . . .

Connor's narrator, Colin, along with cousin Hannah, is encountering the leopard:

> We stumbled up a short hill and then smiled as we gazed along the trunk of a beautiful leadwood tree at the top. The brightly colored leaves, the speckled branches, the red streaks on the trunk, the—swishing tail. We both stopped dead as our eyes locked onto the same spot, putting together the whole picture. The beautiful red streaks were the exaggerated drips of impala blood running down the tree, the beautiful speckles, a leopard. It was swishing its tail and glaring down at us. We felt rooted to the spot, unable to move forward or back, hoping in our hearts that it hadn't yet seen us but knowing that it had. . . . The leopard jumped down the rest of the trunk to come to a stop at the foot, just fifteen yards away from where we were standing. It's funny, but all I was thinking about at that moment was the memory I had had the night before about my childhood fears. About the horrible storms that kept me awake all those nights. I could see its teeth as it yawned again, and I thought of home. I thought of my mother sitting at the kitchen table, tired after all the sleepless nights of worrying, wondering if she would ever find out about us. Resigned to my death, I just hoped for her. For the closure that would never come, the worry that she would feel, the relief she would never feel.

Jess, reading from the second of her heroine's three nightmares, lowers her voice to a dramatic whisper:

I was in the playground at my school again, in the middle of the night. Why am I here? I wondered. Everything around me had seemed to lose saturation, and the transparent wind was so strong that it was almost visible. The swings were rocking back and forth against the sky, and suddenly a bright light started flashing in my direction. I froze. I heard a loud scream from behind a corner in the building, a young girl begging for help. I hid behind the slide. I heard a few cries, each one softer than before. Then they stopped. The light turned off, and I heard footsteps running away at a quick pace, thudding against the pavement. I waited for a few minutes, anxious to see what had happened, although in the back of my mind I already knew. I walked towards the other side of the building. As soon as I turned around, it was clear what had happened.

Her messy black hair covered her entire face, but her body lay limp on the grass, frozen with snow. Her jeans were torn up and her black t-shirt had been cut open by a knife. Blood streamed down her body, originating from her scalp. I moved the hair away from her face, as I held her head in my lap. As I pulled back the strands of black hair, I saw the beginning of intense blue eyes, seeming to look right at me. Her red lips were slightly parted, and her face flushed of all color. At once I realized it was Nicole.

Ayana shyly starts reading her opening, a memory of her father's:

Between 1982 and 1983 I was attending med school in Buffalo, New York. I was living in an apartment building in the area. I had a yellow Audi that I parked on the street right outside the building. One day, shortly after I moved into the neighborhood, I woke up and found my car painted with black letters and the word "nigger" spelt all over it. Interesting thing about this was I was living right next door to the police officer of the Buffalo police department, though I didn't report the incident.

Peter introduces his narrator, who is about to witness an effort by the Greek gods to return and take over the earth:

From my backyard, I watched the stars tonight. It was a clear night, and the Pine Barrens are remote, far from any interfering light. The trees were dark. Venus, she was high in the sky, shining brighter than any star, a pale elegance. The strange thing was, it wasn't supposed to be there. Several Astronomers had calculated exactly how fast it would have to have traveled

to reach its current position, but what's logic worth, anyway? It was there.
To me, as a student of the classics, it had a sort of ominous quality. "Love,"
I thought "and conflict. Don't forget Troy." I sighed and offered a prayer,
just to anyone who was listening, God, Aphrodite, it did not matter. I was
no great professor or historian, as I had once dreamed of being, in the folly
of my youth. I had given all that up, and settled in as a police officer in Egg
Harbor. No wife, no close friends, and now I lived alone out in the woods. I
might as well be as dead as those civilizations I love. "Please let something
happen, before I die of boredom. Prove to me I did not really waste a great
part of my life studying the dead." I ought not to have made such a prayer,
my myths should have taught me that. Venus seemed to glow with pleasure, and I could almost swear I saw the mists on its surface swell and fall,
trailing off to earth, the wisps full of color. And then they were in front of
me, and they congealed, swirling and billowing. And in front of me stood
the most beautiful woman I had ever seen. I do not know how I knew this,
as she was too bright to gaze upon, but it was part of that most immacu-
late presence. A voice rang out, a shimmering diamond, that made all else
mud: "One Worshipper, At Least. That Is Enough For Me. And For Us All."

Taking Stock of the Project

Our celebration fell (was carefully timed to fall) on the day before the winter holidays. The next day I asked the students to assess their experience of
the project using the following questions as a guide:

1. Which pieces that you wrote previous to the free-choice project came in
    useful in creating your project, and why?
2. From what sources did you draw your ideas and inspiration for the project?
    (personal/family experience? imagination/fantasy? news events? movies?
    other?)
3. To what degree did your topic/story line/material/structure change as you
    wrote?
4. What were the most difficult or challenging aspects of the project for you,
    and why?
5. What were the most satisfying aspects, and why?
6. Considering that you sent in the proposal on Dec. 3 and turned in the final
    draft on Dec. 16 (about a two-week span), was there enough time for you?
    Too much? Explain.
7. What do you think you learned—about writing, about yourself—from doing

> this project? And in what ways, if any, do you think your conceiving and
> writing and presenting of it might help you with future writing (in this
> course and elsewhere)?
>
> 8. Do you feel you had enough help when you needed it? Too much? Not
>   enough?
> 9. What kinds of writing have you done this fall in your other courses?

Consensus was clear on certain questions. Yes, the amount of time was exactly right for all but three of the students, and all but two of those three felt
they'd had just the right amount of help—from the mentors, their peers, and
me. Definitely, the best, "most fun, most amazing" part was "getting to write
whatever you wanted," and next year's ninth graders should all get to do
this project. As Jess wrote, "When I heard my peers read from their pieces, I
realized everyone gets to put their heart and soul into this project since they
can write about something they're really passionate about." For some kids,
the fun was in "writing about somebody kind of like me," and for others it
was "making up somebody really different from me." For the profile writers, the interest lay in getting to know someone better whom they already
admired. Yes, everyone found their initial idea took surprising turns as they
wrote, and students found that exciting, for the most part. And nearly everyone recognized that they had taken inspiration from a variety of sources—
primarily life experience, their imaginations, and favorite books, movies,
and TV. While people naturally cited different writing assignments that had
helped them, everyone was able to reference at least one. For many it was
the Holden's Voice narrative, but others mentioned the profile; the personal,
reflective, descriptive nature of their "in the zone" writing; the poems; and
the "issue I'd stand up for" piece. A few cited the poetry. The challenges
mentioned most often included "deciding on the ending," "cutting enough,
not repeating myself, not going over the page limit," and "choosing what to
use from my interviews." Most students felt they'd done very little writing
in other courses except for Spanish, where they enjoyed creating dialogues
with a partner and writing diary entries and a poem. History required essays and a newspaper article; comparative religion, outlines and essays full
of "all the facts you know, the format doesn't matter"; and biology, a research paper on a topic of their choice and lab reports.

What I most wanted to hear was what students thought they had learned
from the project, and the answers to this were varied. Matt: "I learned I

shouldn't be scared to share my paper with the class. It didn't sound cheesy or boring." Ayana: "I learned to take my time instead of hurrying through just to get things done. And that revising is a good tool because before, once I wrote the first draft I thought it was exactly how I wanted it and no one could change it." Connor: "I learned that I can create powerful imagery, and how to make my ideas more concise." Sarah: "That writing can really be fun, you just have to use your imagination." Jess: "I learned more about writing in the first person, which I love. I learned that writing is a great expression of self, when I heard my peers read, and I learned things about them just from their writing. I learned a lot about dialogue and imagery." Peter: "The project definitely helped me better write fiction. I now have more confidence writing this genre." Garret: "I think I can write a longer story now just on my own. Writing is not always a bad thing and can be fun when you choose the right topic." Julia: "I learned about character development and the struggle to make the reader understand the character as well as the writer does." And in addition, many noted that they learned more about time management (including the two students who said there wasn't enough time for this project.)

I myself learned to put a little more faith in kids.

Epilogue: Imaginative Writing, Student Choice, and Standards

When I first contemplated this book, back in 2008, the Common Core State Standards in English Language Arts had not yet been launched, though drafts were appearing. But by now they have been officially adopted by more than forty states, and it's reasonable to ask, once again, "So far/what next?" While my school doesn't have to contend with the standards, I find myself wondering how my students' first semester of writing would help them, by the end of the year, to meet the new Common Core State Writing Standards 9–10. Our students do not take any kind of standardized writing test at the end of ninth grade, so how would I find answers to this question? And how might a teacher who is developing a writing curriculum in a standards-based classroom convince a school administration that writing in many genres, especially the "literary" ones, along with a free-choice project, would help students acquire the skills and experience necessary to achieve core standards?

My efforts at assessment started where I suggest all teachers could start, by asking the students themselves to evaluate their year's progress as writers. After winter break all our ninth graders read Julia Alvarez's semi-historical novel, *In the Time of the Butterflies,* set in the Dominican Republic, about the four Mirabal sisters, three of whom were assassinated under the Trujillo government. My students research and write a three- to five-page paper on some historical or cultural topic relating to the novel and its period, discovering their own lens and their own reasons for the topic's significance to them—the "why it matters, why I care" criterion. They also write a timed essay on which one of the Mirabal sisters strikes them as most courageous. Then for the next four weeks we read and write poetry. In addition to my own writing experience with this genre (Michaels, *Risking Intensity*), I find Kenneth Koch and Kate Farrell's anthology of poems and exercises, *Sleeping on the Wing,* very useful, along with *A Surge of Language: Teaching Poetry Day by Day* by Baron Wormser and David Cappella. Of the eight poems the class writes, they choose four or five for their portfolios, introducing them with a prose *Ars Poetica*—an essay that is both personal and analytical. Then, with poetry in our ears, we move on to *Othello*, staging the midnight brawl scene with the help of an actor-teacher from McCarter, Princeton's regional theater. At the end of this unit, each student chooses a favorite speech, and as they memorize and stage it for the class (or just for me), they write a three-page analysis of the speech and its various functions in the play, beginning with a personal statement about why they chose it. Throughout the year, everyone writes and posts to the class on at least one independent reading book per term and responds online to posts by at least three other students.

Then in June, for the final exam, each writer presents to the rest of us (ideally, in the theater) a piece of any genre, created and performed solo or in collaboration with peers, that investigates a theme present in any four of the works we've read together during the year (one of the four may be a poem). This June, performances range from essays read aloud from the stage, with lighting and a mic, to original monologues in the voices of literary characters, to a scene written, staged, and acted by a foursome—Nick as Hally, Jenna as Emilia from *Othello*, Julia as Minerva Mirabal, and Garret as Holden.

Looking over the final writing assessments students filled out just before the exam (see Figure E.1), I'm interested to hear the confidence behind their comments. Again, as with their responses to the free-choice project, it turns out there's consensus on the favorite assignments: at least 95 percent of the class named the free-choice piece *and* their poetry portfolio. (This is not because I graded those pieces more generously; the class and I had set up demanding assessment criteria for both assignments.) Their views on good writing and on similarities between poetry and prose encourage me to believe that all our work in a variety of genres and with blending personal reflection with research, interviewing, and analysis was paying off. Interestingly, they were not saving "originality" and "imagination" and "emotion" for the literary genres, but felt these qualities were necessary in analytical, persuasive, and research papers as well. (See the College and Career Readiness Core Anchor Standards for Writing, *Note on range and content of student writing*: "[Students] need to know how to combine elements of different

---

Skim through the pieces and comments in your year's portfolio, paying particular attention to your writings from this spring term—your poetry portfolio and *Othello* paper. Then answer the following questions as thoughtfully as you can in full sentences, quoting specific examples from your pieces to support your points:

1. In what areas do you feel you grew the most as a writer this year, and why?
2. When you hear the phrase "good writing," what qualities, techniques, specific pieces, and writers (published and unpublished) come to mind? Explain.
3. What connections do you see between how to write good poems and how to write good prose (essays, stories, scenes, research papers)? What similar skills, talents, processes do they both require?
4. In creating your final exam project, what writing strengths have you drawn on?
5. Of all the pieces you've written this year, which one or two did you enjoy doing the most or feel best about, and why?
6. In what ways have you grown as a peer responder and as a reviser of your own work? How are these two processes similar, and how are they different?
7. What aspects of writing and kinds of writing do you most want to work on next year, and why?
8. Think back over your other courses this year. Describe, briefly, the kinds of writing you've done in them. Are there ways in which any of these kinds of writing have helped you as a writer in general?

FIGURE E.1. *END-OF-YEAR WRITING SELF-ASSESSMENT.*

kinds of writing—for example, to use narrative strategies within argument and explanation within narrative—to produce complex and nuanced writing" [CCSS Initiative, 2010, p. 41].) Many in the class said that both poetry and prose need strong word choices, especially to create images, description, characters, and argument. Some mentioned the importance of sound and rhythm. They said both poetry and prose should try to "captivate" or "draw in" a reader through originality, creativity, strong titles, openings and closings, and honest expression of feelings. And that to do all this, revision was usually necessary. Students recognized that a poem might benefit from revision and editing as much as a critical analysis; poetry, to them, was not simply a spontaneous, inspired overflow of feeling.

In describing "good writing," only a couple of students *focused* on grammar, spelling, and punctuation—unlike those many students who have never experienced a personal investment in their writing and tend to assume success is all about mechanics. James the journalist did, admittedly, emphasize "logical transitions" and accurate citing of quotations, but he also said that good writing is "refined by the writer's concern." Interestingly, Jessica noted that the biggest help in her writing was "just being able to write so much different stuff all year," whereas Ayana said, "Because I *read* so much this year, I know now what good writing is and how to revise mine." Many said they became more critical and honest peer responders, and this helped them in editing their own pieces. But I think I treasure most a comment Peter made—that good writing must be "evocative, persuasive, inspire feeling, make us wonder and care about the characters and ideas . . . like how with *Othello* the tragedy really is tragic for the readers, not merely the end of the book."

As I skimmed the students' portfolios, crammed with profile, zone piece, Holden's Voice, the "something I'd stand up for" argument/narrative, the research paper, personal/critical essay, timed essay, poetry collection, *Othello* speech analysis, and final exam piece, not to mention freewrites, book posts, and various self-assessments and peer responses, I kept a copy of the Common Core State Writing Standards 9–10 next to me, with its heavy emphasis on creating "formal style and objective tone," "arguments to support claims," and "informative/explanatory texts." I was glad that narrative writing had been added to these standards at the end. But still no poetry or theater pieces? I noticed the absence of such verbs as *discover* and *explore*. And above all, the increased emphasis on both reading and writing "informational texts" and "texts to persuade or explain," as opposed to writing "to convey experience" (and feeling). I saw that this was in conformation to the National Assessment of Educational Progress's increasing emphasis on informational reading and writing: ". . . the overwhelming focus of writing throughout high school should be on arguments and informative/explanatory texts." There it was again: "texts." Should flesh-and-blood teenagers really be asked to produce "texts"? All this in the service of making them "ready for college, workforce training, and life in a technological society." To prepare them "to produce and consume media," a need for which "is embedded into every aspect of today's curriculum." What about becoming participatory citizens of a democracy? Loyal friends? Caring and effective partners and parents? And then I noticed, finally, tucked away at the end of this "Introduction to Key Design Considerations," one admission that particularly struck me: that the language arts standards do not try to provide for "attention to such matters as social, emotional and physical development and approaches to learning"—which the authors allow is important "particularly in the early grades." Not important for teenagers?

I returned to the portfolios, trying to ignore their young writers' preoccupation with social, emotional, and physical development and to focus on whether the first half-year of writing had made any significant impact on the second. What had students learned? What could I show an administrator? A supervisor? And as I read, I thought for the millionth time how ninth graders are such an amazing mix of child and growing adult. The writers of these 9–10 standards allowed as how by the end of tenth grade a student writer should be at a higher level of sophistication in his manipulation of skills than a ninth grader. Perhaps that meant a ninth grader could get away with writing more out of personal experience and feeling, out of imagination and playfulness? "Shades of the prison house" might be held off for a little? But indeed, my writers were learning how to use and organize information—whether obtained through interviews; observation of themselves; invented details about characters, setting, and action; analyses of other writers' characters and language; or researched facts. During this year, I could see them, through their portfolios, discovering the pleasures of precise and sensory language—particularly through writing poetry, description, reflection, narrative; recognizing the need for a clear sequence of events or ideas, of subordinating one point to another; struggling with the challenge of choosing and maintaining a point of view; confronting choices: of shifting tenses (or not), of changing pace, of creating (or avoiding) transitions, of taking poetic license with punctuation or paragraphing or sentence structure. . . . Pretty much all the Common Core State Writing Standards 9–10.

However, the students had done all this not to meet a set of nationally imposed requirements but to satisfy goals and criteria that they had set, together with me, out of their growing discovery of themselves as writers. The Common Core State Standards argue for "an integrated model of literacy," noting that, for example, Writing Standard 9 requires that students be able to write about what they read. They don't mention that students can become more insightful readers by reading what they write—again and again, silently, aloud, to themselves and to their peers. And by starting to read other texts, from *Catcher in the Rye* to *Othello*, as *writers*.

I choose two portfolios, not entirely at random: Jordan's and James's. A weak writer and a strong one, to judge from their grades. A boy being raised by one parent plus extended family and a boy from a two-parent family, whose father is a teacher at our school. An African American boy and a European American boy. A boy new to our school and one who's been here most of his life. Plenty of stereotypes, but I want to focus on ways in which each student's first half-year of writing contributed to the second half.

Jordan's second piece of the year, the "in the zone" description, hooks us right away: "How could I not be in the zone? This was the championship game. The pressure of winning was controlling my body all week." Note the question to the reader, the short sentence following it, and then the physical sensation, which also shifts the time frame briefly from the immediate moment to the gradual buildup of tension during the past week. This feels like instinctive writing, natural to a kid who's personally committed to his topic. The piece proceeds pretty much chronologically through the events and sensations of the game. A month later Jordan's entering Holden Caulfield's voice. He tries hooking us with a typically Holden exaggeration, "It was the phoniest day of my life," and moves right into the moment: "The Peer Group leaders were there pretending to give a damn about us. They were just doing it for their goddam credits and all." Then an immediate sensation: "It was very cold outside too. I thought I had pneumonia, it was so cold and my hair was wet." And then the first event in the day's sequence, a sequence that Jordan as Holden will interrupt from time to time by digressing to various obsessive loves and fears: "This crappy day started at the Princeton Battlefield, where we began with some group discussion. We all had to talk about that touchy feely personal crap. Like what do you enjoy about your family and stuff." Then on to his little sister Phoebe. A few weeks later, Jordan is writing about "something you'd stand up for." Here he tries a somewhat more distanced stance for his opening, though by the second sentence we see how personal the topic is for him. (Probably Jordan's strength as a writer will always lie in finding a personal connection to his material, as he observes in his final writing assessment and as we'll see him do later in his research paper and his *Othello* paper, but he has three more years in which to learn to detach for more formal pieces.) "As history shows," he writes, "racism was never dead and no matter what has happened [this was just before Obama's election] it is still heavily out in the world today. How do people think that they have the right to say Blacks are not as good as them? My grandparents, great grandparents, and even my parents had to go through this. My dad always shares this story of when he and his friends . . ."

I jump seven months ahead to the paper analyzing a speech from *Othello*. I'm focusing on Jordan's openings because one of his consistent problems is sustaining concentration and energy through an entire piece; what he *has* learned is the importance of starting off strongly and clearly:

> Are any of us ever in the right frame of mind? We have mind battles constantly when we have to make decisions. That's a risk we take. Othello too had a decision; his was manipulated by Iago and couldn't have been more wrong. What drew me to this speech (V. ii. 115–117) is the way Othello's mind is going back and forth. It is spoken with very choppy sentences, so it's visible that he's almost lost his mind.

Again, the approach is personal, but Jordan has pulled back far enough to consider "any of us," to use the second-person plural. Despite his yearlong difficulty in writing gracefully about literature, not an unusual problem for fourteen-year-old boys, his voice is brisk and confident (and he's finally learned how to use the semicolon!). He's also paying attention—though perhaps too early in the paper, thereby blurring his focus a bit—to the sound of the sentence structure through which Shakespeare reveals Othello's mental state, an observation Jordan certainly couldn't have made before our first foray into poetry writing back in the fall. In his second paragraph, I see he's integrating a quotation with his context and follow-up sentences, something he first learned to do in his profile on Connor back in September:

> In this scene Othello has just killed Desdemona and now he is contemplat-
> ing what he just did, when Emilia walks in. Othello's talking aloud but in
> his head about Emilia coming inside the bedroom. "Yes. 'Tis Emilia.—By
> and by.—She's dead. 'Tis like she comes to speak of Cassio's death. The
> noise was here. Ha, no more moving? Still as the grave. Shall she come in?
> Were't good? I think she stirs again. No. What's best to do?" (V. ii. 115–117).
> He is going back and forth thinking about what he should do and basically
> seems crazy.

While Jordan hasn't mastered the rules for handling a block quotation of poetry, he's set up context for it, used it clearly as textual evidence, and cited it accurately. Without the first term's varied writing assignments that were more congenial to him and came more naturally—without the interest he developed then in hooking a reader, sequencing clearly to serve the different purposes of his pieces, physicalizing experience, and incorporating specific details as evidence—I can't imagine Jordan completing an analysis of a passage from Shakespeare with any degree of success at all. He had also found the mid-winter research paper difficult, partly due to his having chosen a complex topic about two failed attempts against Trujillo's government, but even there he was motivated to get started by a personal focus: "Imagine not being free. Unable to have the opportunity to do what you thought was right."

I turn to James's portfolio. Unlike Jordan, he's comfortable with sequencing ideas clearly and generally sustains his concentration throughout his pieces. For him, the challenge has been to allow his feelings and personal experiences to surface. He's grown up admiring his father, the history teacher, for a cool, sometimes witty, detached mastery of reason and fact. But James has his passions, tennis and theater among them. Back in the fall his zone piece, about tennis, began with sound and image:

> I can hear words of encouragement and tactics from my coach, but her
> voice is lost, unimportant. I already know. There are no surprises, this
> is perfection and even if I tried I couldn't mess it up. Every movement
> I make is the right one, and each shot is effortless and exactly where I
> planned it to be. The grip of the racket seems natural, and the racket be-
> comes a part of me. . . . I feel each quiver the racket makes, as I send the
> ball back over the net.

Evident here, in the tennis and the writing—and elsewhere in his theater dancing—James has a wonderful sense of rhythm, for the power of repetition, of parallelism. The sequence of physical and state-of-mind details serves the piece beautifully. Is it instinctive? Not entirely. By his November self-assessment, James was noting that he had learned to edit his writing *aloud*. Looking at his *Othello* paper written seven months later, I see that too begins with a focus on sound and an image that physicalizes Othello's effort to forget his love for Desdemona. James seems to have learned from his earlier writings that this can be a powerful way to open a piece: "'All my fond love thus do I blow to heaven. / 'Tis gone' (III.iii.505–6)." James goes on to explain: "I was drawn to this particular speech because of the language as well as the images Shakespeare uses. Othello uses very strong nouns and verbs with hard consonants like 'tyrannous hate' and 'blow,' and reading this passage aloud enforces the power of Othello's words." Then the actor in James emerges, with his sense of the whole speech's physicality and passion: "I also thought that it would be an exciting speech to perform because of its energy. . . . [H]e reinforces his hatred for Desdemona and Cassio and wholly satisfies the reader that he is mad with jealousy."

James wrestled with sequencing his ideas back in the September profile, where we discussed in class (Chapter 2) ways to move back and forth through time. His profile of Peter's love of biking on the boardwalk starts by establishing the routine: "<u>Every morning in the summer</u> you can find Peter biking on the boardwalk at Ocean City, New Jersey. Peter's been going to Ocean City <u>since he was two years old</u>. In fact, he <u>first traversed</u> the boardwalk in 'one of those attachable things' on the back of his father's bike." Then there's a slightly awkward time shift from continuous present to the moment of the interview, to accommodate a quoted observation from Peter: "He <u>makes stops</u> at the arcades and for a diet Pepsi along the boardwalk, <u>adding that</u> the morning journey is 'one of my favorite activities, definitely.'" But already James is learning to use time—and rhythm—effectively in moving to a natural conclusion: "A voice echoes across the boardwalk; 'It is now 12 noon. All bicycles off the boardwalk.'" By the late fall's free-choice project, he is moving back and forth, in a five-page profile, between a chronological account of his grandfather's six-month job counseling and helping to select astronauts, quotations from interviews with his grandfather, and James's own reflections on this story. Two months later, in his timed essay on Minerva Mirabal's courage, he's making smooth transitions through a chronological account of how Alvarez shows the courage developing: "even as a child and adolescent . . . from the first, she begins . . . after she graduates she succeeds . . . Until after her stint in jail, Minerva personifies . . . Minerva eventually becomes . . ." More impressively, James moves to a conclusion that weighs claim and counterclaim: "Minerva's courage is one that is unequaled in Alvarez's novel, but with this courage come both negative and positive consequences. . . ."

James's combination of logic and a good ear helped him develop into a writer of effective conclusions that flow naturally from thesis or opening scene and leave us with a satisfying sense of closure—a sense that we have made a journey. Finding a point of sonic and logical rest in "All bicycles off the boardwalk," and in his zone piece ending, "Game, set, match," James moved on to a shattering insight about his fear to stand up for a friend: "The next day I apologized to him. . . . He understood my dilemma, but my inability to act must have made believing me much more difficult." His research paper on Trujillo's rise to power ends with effective summation of his findings, subordinating the dictator's positive side to his immorality: "The reasons for support of him were mixed. The US wanted a strong ruler who would speak out against communism and bolster the economy, which Trujillo provided. Other backers of Trujillo supported him for the modernization of the country. However, the means by which he obtained this power were corrupt, to say the least. The president of a country should be an honorable person, and Trujillo was anything but." And, finally, James's essay on *Othello* concludes: "This speech from Othello truly does signify a turning point in his development as a character. He commits to killing both Cassio and Desdemona, consuming himself with jealousy. Othello marks his words at the end of his speech, saying, 'In the due reverence of a sacred vow, / I here engage my words' (III, iii, 523–524). Othello pushes his radical belief in Desdemona and Cassio's affair over the edge—there's no going back now." James commented on this particular conclusion: "My closing could have been more descriptive."

Looking over the Common Core State Writing Standards 9–10 once more, simply in light of these two portfolios, and skimming the Standards for Language as well, I can see that both Jordan and James have made valuable progress in all the areas required, though in some more than others. And I can't imagine their having the confidence, skills, and motivation to tackle the research, analytical, and reflective papers of the second semester without having begun to discover the skills and challenges they did in our first half-year of writing. Their self-assessments support this conviction. The class as a whole seemed to agree that "all good writing is creative," whether poetry or prose, narrative or expository. As teachers we need to remind ourselves: The authors of the Common Core State Standards have made it clear that *we* are to design whatever curriculum, tools, and approaches to learning we think can best help our students meet these standards. We are the ones who know these students: their social, emotional, and physical needs, the environments and families from which they come, their conflicting desires to be and speak for themselves as individuals yet to find a community—for writing and for other kinds of support—where they can feel at home. We know they are more likely to keep coming to school and to thrive there together if, as Katherine Paterson says, we can help them perform their fundamental task as human beings—exercising the imagination in order to seek connection with others. We know, from our own experience as students and our struggles as teachers, that her description of the basic task of education as "the care and feeding of the imagination" sets the bar high. With help from our students, we need to ensure, in our own classrooms with our own methods, that we reach the temporary journey's end in June feeling we have fed the imaginations under our care.

Works Cited

Alvarez, Julia. *In the Time of the Butterflies*. New York: Plume-Penguin, 1995. Print.

Atwell, Nancie. *The Reading Zone: How to Help Kids Become Skilled, Passionate, Habitual, Critical Readers*. New York: Scholastic, 2007. Print.

Burroway, Janet. *Writing Fiction: A Guide to Narrative Craft*. 5th ed. New York: Longman, 2000. Print.

Collins, Billy, ed. *180 More: Extraordinary Poems for Every Day*. New York: Random, 2005. Print.

Common Core State Standards Initiative. "English Language Arts Standards." *Common Core State Standards Initiative*. 2010. Web. 29 June 2011.

Csikszentmihalyi, Mihaly. *Creativity: Flow and the Psychology of Discovery and Invention*. New York: Harper, 1996. Print.

Cummings, E. E. *Poems, 1923–1954*. New York: Harcourt, 1954. Print.

Dean, Deborah. *Strategic Writing: The Writing Process and Beyond in the Secondary English Classroom*. Urbana, IL: NCTE, 2006. Print.

Doty, Mark. Turtle, Swan *and* Bethlehem in Broad Daylight: *Two Volumes of Poetry*. Chicago: U of Illinois P, 2000. Print.

Fletcher, Ralph. *What a Writer Needs*. Portsmouth, NH: Heinemann, 1993. Print.

Fugard, Athol. *"Master Harold"... and the boys*. New York: Penguin, 1982. Print.

———. *Notebooks, 1960–1977*. New York: Theatre Communications, 1983. Print.

Golub, Jeffrey N. *Making Learning Happen: Strategies for an Interactive Classroom*. Portsmouth, NH: Boynton/Cook, 2000. Print.

Graves, Donald H. *Writing: Teachers and Children at Work*. 20th anv. ed. Portsmouth, NH: Heinemann, 2003. Print.

Hacker, Diana. *A Writer's Reference*. 5th ed. Boston: Bedford/St. Martin's, 2003. Print.

Heard, Georgia. *For the Good of the Earth and Sun: Teaching Poetry*. Portsmouth, NH: Heinemann, 1989. Print.

Jago, Carol. *Beyond Standards: Excellence in the High School English Classroom*. Portsmouth, NH: Boynton/Cook, 2001. Print.

———. *Cohesive Writing: Why Concept Is Not Enough*. Portsmouth, NH: Heinemann, 2002. Print.

Koch, Kenneth, and Kate Farrell, eds. *Sleeping on the Wing: An Anthology of Modern Poetry with Essays on Reading and Writing*. New York: Vintage-Random, 1982. Print.

Le Guin, Ursula K. *Steering the Craft: Exercises and Discussions on Story Writing for the Lone Navigator or the Mutinous Crew*. Portland, OR: Eighth Mountain, 1998. Print.

Lincoln Center Institute. *Aesthetic Education, Inquiry, and the Imagination*. New York: Lincoln Center for the Performing Arts, 2007. Print.

MICHAELS, JUDITH ROWE. *Dancing With Words: Helping Students Love Language through Authentic Vocabulary Instruction*. Urbana, IL: NCTE, 2001. Print.

———. *Risking Intensity: Reading and Writing Poetry with High School Students.* Urbana, IL: NCTE, 1999. Print.

MURRAY, DONALD M. *Crafting a Life: In Essay, Story, Poem.* Portsmouth, NH: Boynton/ Cook, 1996. Print.

NYE, NAOMI SHIHAB. *Words under the Words: Selected Poems*. Portland, OR: Eighth Mountain: 1995. Print.

OBAMA, BARAK. *Dreams from My Father: A Story of Race and Inheritance.* New York: Crown, 2004. Print.

PATERSON, KATHERINE. *The Spying Heart: More Thoughts on Reading and Writing Books for Children*. New York: Lodestar Books/Dutton, 1989. Print.

PIRIE, BRUCE. *Teenage Boys and High School English*. Portsmouth, NH: Heinemann, 2002. Print.

QUINDLEN, ANNA. "The Eye of the Reporter, the Heart of the Novelist." Writers on Writing column. *New York Times* 23 Sept. 2002. Print.

RIEF, LINDA. *Seeking Diversity: Language Arts with Adolescents.* Portsmouth, NH: Heinemann Educational Books, 1992. Print.

ROMANO, TOM. *Crafting Authentic Voice*. Portsmouth, NH: Heinemann, 2004. Print.

———. "The Danger of Countenance." *English Journal* 92.6 (2003): 26–30.

SALINGER, J. D. *The Catcher in the Rye*. New York: Back Bay-Little, 2001. Print.

SIPE, REBECCA BOWERS. *Adolescent Literacy at Risk? The Impact of Standards*. Urbana, IL: NCTE, 2009. Print.

Slouka, Mark. "Dehumanized: When Math and Science Rule the School." *Harper's Magazine* Sept. 2009: 32–40. Print.

Smith, Anna Deavere. *Letters to a Young Artist: Straight-up Advice on Making a Life in the Arts—For Actors, Performers, Writers, and Artists of Every Kind*. New York: Anchor-Random, 2006. Print.

Smith, Michael W., and Jeffrey D. Wilhelm. "*Reading Don't Fix No Chevys*": *Literacy in the Lives of Young Men*. Portsmouth, NH: Heinemann, 2002. Print.

Stevens, Wallace. *The Collected Poems*. New York: Vintage, 1990. Print.

Tunstall, Tricia. *Note by Note: A Celebration of the Piano Lesson*. New York: Simon, 2008. Print.

Welty, Eudora. *One Writer's Beginnings*. Cambridge: Harvard UP, 1995. Print.

Williams, William Carlos. *Selected Poems*. Ed. Charles Tomlinson. New York: New Directions, 1985. Print.

Wormser, Baron, and David Cappella. *A Surge of Language: Teaching Poetry Day by Day*. Portsmouth, NH: Heinemann, 2004. Print.

Zinsser, William. *On Writing Well: An Informal Guide to Writing Nonfiction*. 4th ed. New York: Harper, 1990. Print.

Author

Photo courtesy of Sybil Holland.

For 43 years a high school English teacher in public and independent schools and currently writer in residence K–12 at Princeton Day School in Princeton, New Jersey, Dr. Judith Rowe Michaels has written two books for NCTE, *Risking Intensity* (1999) and *Dancing with Words* (2001), and two collections of poetry, *The Forest of Wild Hands* (University Press of Florida, 2001) and *Reviewing the Skull* (WordTech Editions, 2010). Her poems have appeared in such journals as *Poetry, Poetry Northwest, Yankee, The Women's Review of Books, Nimrod, Calyx, The New York Quarterly,* and *The Literary Review*. Several of her articles have been published in *English Journal,* and she has presented on poetry at conferences around the country. Michaels was a consultant on teacher outreach for two of PBS's poetry series with Bill Moyers, *The Language of Life* and *Fooling with Words,* as well as for the satellite broadcast from the 1998 Dodge Poetry Festival. For many years, she has served as poet in the schools for the Geraldine R. Dodge Foundation. She has received two poetry fellowships from the New Jersey State Council on the Arts and been nominated for three

Pushcart Prizes. Michaels is a founding member of Cool Women, a poetry critique, performance, and publishing collective. A 14-year cancer survivor, she presents on ovarian cancer at New Jersey and New York City medical schools through Survivors Teaching Students, Saving Women's Lives, a program now in more than 70 medical schools across the country.

Catching Tigers in Red Weather

Composed by Barbara Frazier in Veljovic and ExPonto.
The typeface used on the cover is Optima.
Calligraphy by Barbara Yale-Read.
Printed by Versa Press, Inc. on 50-lb. Opaque Offset paper.